RME
for Scotland

Joe Walker

The Publishers would like to thank the following for permission to reproduce copyright material:

Photo credits
Page 2 © Lucasfilm/20th Century Fox/The Kobal Collection; page 3 (top) © Chip Simons/Science Faction/Corbis; page 4 © SuperStock/Getty Images; page 6 (top) © Chip Simons/ Science Faction/Corbis, (bottom) © Robert Harding Picture Library Ltd/Alamy; page 7 © Red Images, LLC/Alamy; page 9 (top) © Gavin MacVicar/ iStockphoto, (bottom) © Chip Simons/Science Faction/Corbis; page 10 © NASA Jet Propulsion Laboratory; page 11 © Chip Simons/Science Faction/Corbis; page 12 © Poncho/Getty Images; page 13 © Matjaz Tancic/Alamy; page 15 (top) © Keystone/Getty Images, (bottom) © Imagestate Media; page 16 © Chip Simons/Science Faction/Corbis; page 18 © (top) Anders Blomqvist/Getty Images, (bottom) © Photodisc/Getty Images; page 19 © Photodisc/Photolibrary Group Ltd; page 20 © Art Directors & TRIP/Alamy; page 22 (top) © Bill Miller/Alamy, (bottom) © Imagestate Media; page 23 © Pep Roig/Alamy; page 24 © H. Mark Weidman Photography/Alamy; page 25 (top) © Steve Sant/Alamy, (bottom) © Photodisc/ Getty Images; page 26 By permission of Egmont Publishing Group; page 28 (top) © Christian Kapteyn/Alamy, (bottom) © Purestock/Photolibrary Group Ltd; page 30 (top) © Gavin Gough/ Alamy, (left) © Brooklyn Museum/Corbis, (right) © Purestock/Photolibrary Group Ltd; page 32 © M L Pearson/Alamy; page 34 © Rick Gomez/Blend Images/Corbis; page 35 (top) © Trinity Mirror/Mirrorpix/Alamy, (bottom) © Veronique de Viguerie/Getty Images; page 37 (top) © Design Pics Inc./Alamy, (bottom) © Wendy Stone/Corbis; page 38 © Design Pics Inc./ Alamy; page 39 © Ann Johansson/Corbis; page 40 © Marco Secchi/Rex Features; page 41 © Alistair Devine/Getty Images; page 42 © Michael Willis/Alamy; page 43 © Juniors Bildarchiv/Alamy; page 44 © Christopher Furlong/Getty Images; page 45 © Jaipal Singh/epa/Corbis; page 46 © mediacolor's/Alamy; page 47 (top) Private Collection/Peter Newark American Pictures/The Bridgeman Art Library, (bottom) © Yahya Arhab/epa/Corbis; page 50 © Travel Division Images/Alamy; page 51 © Christopher Furlong/Getty Images; page 53 © Gregory Wrona/ Alamy; page 54 (bottom) © ICP-UK/Alamy; page 55 © Karen Minasyan/AFP/Getty Images; page 56 © Purestock/Photolibrary Group Ltd; page 57 © PhotoSpin, Inc/Alamy; page 58 © Michael Melford/National Geographic/Getty Images; page 59 © Art Directors & TRIP/Alamy; page 60 © Eye Ubiquitous/Alamy; page 61 (top) © Tim Gainey/Alamy, (bottom) © World Religions Photo Library/Alamy; page 62 © Picture Partners/Alamy; page 63 © Martin Norris/ Alamy; page 67 © Rolf Richardson/Alamy; page 68 © Dreamworks/The Kobal Collection; page 69 (both) © Louise Murray/Photolibrary; page 70 © Little Brown, Book Group 2003; page 72 © Akademie der Bildenden Künste, Vienna, Austria/The Bridgeman Art Library; page 73 (top) © SuperStock/Getty Images, (bottom) © Malane Newman/Getty Images; page 74 © Eddie Gerald/Alamy; page 76 © WoodyStock/Alamy; page 77 © Ville Palonen/Alamy; page 78 © Courtesy of the British Humanist Association (BHA); page 79 © Courtesy of Prometheus Books (Amherst, NY); www.prometheusbooks.com; page 80 © Lilyana Vynogradova/Alamy; page 82 (top) © Imagestate Media, (bottom) © Stockbyte/Getty Images; page 83 © Rungroj Yongrit/epa/Corbis; page 85 © Siqui Sanchez/Getty Images; page 86 (top) © imagebroker/ Alamy, (bottom) © BUAV; page 88 © Imagestate Media; page 89 © Trinity Mirror/Mirrorpix/Alamy; page 90 © Stockbyte/Getty Images; page 94 © Imagestate Media; page 95 (top) © Borderlands/Alamy, (bottom) © Stockbyte/Getty Images; page 96 © Arnd Wiegmann/Reuters/Corbis; page 98 © Siri Stafford/Getty Images; page 99 Mikael Utterström/Alamy; page 100 © Peter Treanor/Alamy; page 101 © NASA, ESA, and the Hubble Heritage Team (STScI/AURA) - ESA/Hubble Collaboration; page 102 (top) © Derek Croucher/Alamy, (bottom) By permission of Hodder & Stoughton in partnership with Windblown Media; page 103 © Stan Pritchard/Alamy; page 104 © Niall Carson/PA Wire/Press Association Images; page 105 © Photodisc/Getty Images; page 106 © Catchlight Visual Services/Alamy; page 107 © Catchlight Visual Services/Alamy; page 108 (top) © Gianni Giansanti/Immaginazione/ Corbis, (bottom) © David Lees/Corbis; page 109 © Derek Blair/PA Archive/Press Association Images; page 110 (right) © Garntec Images/Alamy; page 111 (top) © Photodisc/Getty Images, (bottom) © Peter Horree/Alamy; page 112 © Mariana Bazo/Reuters/Corbis; page 114 © Ancient Art & Architecture Collection Ltd/Alamy; page 115 © Dorling Kindersley/Getty Images; page 116 (top) © Private Collection/© Look and Learn/The Bridgeman Art Library, (bottom) By permission of Terry Pratchett and Stephen Briggs; page 117 © Penny Tweedie/ Corbis; page 118 © Bill Bachman/Alamy; page 120 © Bible Society, London/The Bridgeman Art Library; page 121 (top) Peter Barritt/Alamy, (bottom) © Pascal Deloche/Godong/Corbis; page 122 © Sandy Huffaker/Getty Images; page 123 © Mehau Kulyk/Science Photo Library; page 124 © Kimberly White/Reuters/Corbis; page 126 © Pictorial Press Ltd/Alamy; page 127 © Christian Jegou Publiphoto Diffusion/Science Photo Library; page 128 © David Gifford/ Science Photo Library; page 130 © WoodyStock/Alamy; page 131 (bottom) © T.M.O. Buildings/Alamy; page 132 © Libby Welch/Alamy Libby Welch/Alamy; page 134 © Alexander Nemenov/AFP/Getty Images; page 135 © STR/AFP/Getty Images; page 136 (left) © Art Directors & TRIP/Alamy, (right) By permission of The Salvation Army; page 137 (top) © World Religions Photo Library/Alamy, (bottom) By permission of The Salvation Army; page 139 (both top) Courtesy Christian Aid and Johnson Banks, (both bottom) Courtesy Christian Aid; page 140 © Sion Touhig/Corbis; page 142 (left) Courtesy Save the Children, (right) Courtesy Age UK; page 143 Courtesy Save the Children (photo: Anna Kari); page 144 © Images of India/Alamy; page 146 © Mike Voss/Alamy; page 147 (bottom) © Pinto/Corbis; page 148 © LWA-Dann Tardif/Corbis; page 153 (top) © Photodisc/Getty Images, (bottom) © Corbis; page 154 © Allstar Picture Library/Alamy; page 156 © Atef Hassan/Reuters/Corbis; page 157 © Horizon International Images Limited/Alamy; page 158 © NASA Goddard Space Flight Center (NASA-GSFC); page 159 (top) © Photodisc/ Photolibrary Group Ltd, (bottom) © Frans Lanting/Corbis.
All other photos © Hodder Gibson.

Acknowledgements
The author would like to thank Lorna and David as ever for their patience, understanding and support during this project and during the whole process of developing RME in the CfE programme.

The author would also like to thank colleagues across the country into whose classes he was privileged to be allowed entry while Development Officer for RME for LTS, and especially those whose responses, reviews and other work were instrumental in helping CfE RME become what it is.

Finally, thanks again to all the pupils in RME classes at Liberton High School who are more often than not test subjects for various ideas and approaches which usually end up in a textbook somewhere...

Every effort has been made to trace all copyright holders, but if any have been inadvertently overlooked the Publishers will be pleased to make the necessary arrangements at the first opportunity.

Although every effort has been made to ensure that website addresses are correct at time of going to press, Hodder Gibson cannot be held responsible for the content of any website mentioned in this book. It is sometimes possible to find a relocated web page by typing in the address of the home page for a website in the URL window of your browser.

Hachette UK's policy is to use papers that are natural, renewable and recyclable products and made from wood grown in sustainable forests. The logging and manufacturing processes are expected to conform to the environmental regulations of the country of origin.

Orders: please contact Bookpoint Ltd, 130 Milton Park, Abingdon, Oxon OX14 4SB. Telephone: (44) 01235 827720. Fax: (44) 01235 400454. Lines are open 9.00 – 5.00, Monday to Saturday, with a 24-hour message answering service. Visit our website at www.hoddereducation.co.uk. Hodder Gibson can be contacted direct on: Tel: 0141 848 1609; Fax: 0141 889 6315; email: hoddergibson@hodder.co.uk

Cover photo © Gavin MacVicar/iStockphoto.com (left); © MShep2/iStockphoto.com (middle); © The Art Gallery Collection/Alamy (right)
Illustrations by Metaphrog
Typeset in FS Albert Light 11.5/14.5 pt by Pantek Arts Ltd, Maidstone, Kent
Printed in Italy

A catalogue record for this title is available from the British Library

ISBN: 978 1444 11074 6

Contents

Contents mapping grid

Introduction

Contents mapping grid

Topic	Beliefs	Values and issues	Practices and traditions	Development of beliefs and values
1. Beliefs **1** What is belief? **2** Ancient and modern beliefs **3** Religious belief: does it matter? **4** Types of belief **5** Exploring belief	✓			✓
2. Exploring Buddhism **6** The Buddha **7** The Four Noble Truths **8** The Eightfold Path **9** Meditation **10** Buddhist art	✓	✓	✓	✓
3. Human rights **11** The right of the child **12** The right to an education **13** The right of free speech **14** The right to economic security **15** The rights of women	✓	✓	✓	✓
4. Winter celebrations **16** Hogmanay **17** Christmas **18** Hanukkah **19** Diwali **20** Samhain	✓		✓	✓
5. Philosophical issues **21** Views about life after death **22** Heaven and Hell **23** Judgement Day **24** Reincarnation/rebirth **25** Humanist perspectives	✓	✓		✓

Introduction

This book explores CfE Religious and Moral Education by suggesting topics and ways of approaching the requirements which cover all of the outcomes and experiences (and more) at Level 3.

The Curriculum for Excellence development programme had as one of its central tenets the idea of flexibility for schools and communities as well as individual teachers. Teachers and schools should respond to their own contexts and students in ways which result in quality learning and teaching experiences which are enjoyed by all. The key to good learning and teaching is **quality**. Quite literally, 'it ain't what you do; it's the way that you do it'.

CfE RME effectively has three modes of operating:

- starting with the student and his or her own exploration and analysis of their own beliefs, values and practices
- moving out to the wider community locally and nationally and comparing and contrasting these with the student's own developing beliefs and values
- finally widening out into a global context over time and place thus orienting the student in terms of their own place in the world and therefore their own possible contribution to it.

This means extending learning beyond the local and national context – out into the wider world – and stressing the interconnected nature of our world and the role which all of us can play in making it a better one. This book is therefore a proposed way to go about RME, but it is expected that teachers will adapt the contained resources to suit their needs and the needs of their students in their own context. The aim of this book is to spark your creativity, not box it in.

Each section of the book follows this format:

An **active introductory stimulus** section destined to engage students and get them thinking about the topic area they're about to explore. It's meant to be humorous but not flippant – and it would be best experienced by students themselves, not just by their teacher reading it to them. It would be expected that this should start off discussion and thinking and the whole process of critical reflection.

A **talking and listening** section. This should come right after the stimulus and should be used to help students think about their own responses to the issues raised, express them and also to listen to what's being expressed by others in the class.

A brief bit of **informative text**. This is intentionally brief as this book offers a more exploratory and active approach to learning. This text should be seen as a natural extension of the talking and listening section.

An **active learning** section. This is designed to encourage students to take ownership of their own learning, exploring and reflecting on their learning as they go.

A **progress check** section. This follows the broad principles of 'Assessment for Learning' and is designed to assess learning in active and creative ways, focusing on knowledge, understanding, analysis, evaluation and skills such as critical thinking and reflection.

An **on your own** section. This is designed so that students engage in independent learning activities. These are not just 'finding out more' tasks but ideas which allow students to explore the topics in a variety of ways.

RME should be enjoyable, informative and life-changing (just like all education). Importantly it should help make the world a better place. Thank you for your contributions in helping your students to do just that.

Joe Walker

1

Beliefs

1 What is belief?

Edmund is one of those people with a clipboard who stops you in the street and asks you questions. One week he's asking you to support a charity, the next he's asking you where you buy your clothes. Today he has to ask people about their beliefs. His day is about to get interesting...

Ed: Morning sir, may I ask you a few questions?

Man 1: [*Very calm, but staring quite directly at Edmund*] Of course you may, young Paduan.

Ed: Would you be prepared to tell me a little bit about your beliefs?

Man 1: Of course. I am a Jedi Knight.

Ed: [*Can't find a box to tick on his clipboard*] Eh ... I see ... I'll put that down as 'Other', shall I?

Man 1: As you please, although there are at least 390,000 of us, and we are a religion officially recognised by the British Government.

Ed: So, your main beliefs are...?

Man 1: That the cosmic energy of the Force comes with a good side and a dark side, and that this influences all life-forms in the Universe.

Ed: So this is the Obi Wan Kenobi, Luke Skywalker thing from the movies?

Man 1: That is one representation, yes.

Ed: Well ... eh ... thank you for that ... have a nice day.

Man 1: Be mindful my child, and may the Force be with you.

Ed: [*Scribbles on his clipboard and approaches another person*] Hi, can I ask you about your beliefs?

Woman 1: Yes, I follow Pastafarianism.

Ed: Shouldn't that be Rastafarianism?

Woman 1: No, I'm a Pastafarian, I'm a member of the Church of the Flying Spaghetti Monster.

Ed: What is a Flying Spaghetti Monster? Does such a thing really exist?

Woman 1: Some Pastafarians think so and others don't. We don't really worry too much about it because you can't prove it either way. So we just get on with our lives as best we can.

Ed: So you don't have any beliefs, really.

Woman 1: Oh I do. I believe that humans have evolved from pirates. Do you know that we share 99.9 per cent of our DNA with pirates?

Ed: Thanks ... very much. I need to move on now...

Woman 1: You're welcome, may you be touched by the Flying Spaghetti Monster's noodly appendage.

Ed: [*Obviously feeling pretty weird now, he approaches a third person nervously*] Morning! Can I take a little time to ask about your beliefs today?

Man 2: Yes, I believe there's a pink teapot orbiting the Earth.

Ed: Eh ... can you see this with an ordinary telescope or do you need a fancy one?

Man 2: Don't be silly – the teapot is completely invisible...

Beliefs

Yes, Jedi is now an official religion that is recognised in England and Wales. Based on census information, seven out of every 1000 people claim to be a Jedi. And yes, the Church of the Flying Spaghetti Monster exists. And finally, maybe there is a pink teapot orbiting the Earth – because if it's invisible then we can't disprove it or prove it.

People believe all sorts of things throughout the world. Some of these beliefs might seem quite normal to us and others might seem really weird – but who's to say what makes a belief normal or not? Sometimes beliefs are based on evidence, but sometimes they are based on a particular experience or because something just 'feels' right. Perhaps we believe things because our parents brought us up to do so, or because everyone else around us does. Sometimes our beliefs go against what everyone else thinks. Our beliefs can be very important to us – in fact, they can shape our whole lives. They have also shaped the history of our world – for better or for worse. What beliefs do you have? Why do you have them?

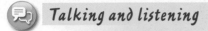

Talking and listening

- What do you think about the beliefs Edmund has heard?
- What do you believe in (or not)?
- Some people are ready to die for their beliefs. Does that make sense?
- Could there be an invisible pink teapot orbiting the Earth?
- What beliefs are there in your class?

Active Learning

1. Think about the things that you believe in. Now fill a box with objects that give clues about your beliefs. For example, if you follow a religion, you could put in an object linked to it. Share your boxes with the class – can your classmates work out what you believe from the objects in the box?

2. Where do people's beliefs 'come from'? Here are some ideas. Think about how each one might influence the things you believe in. Can you come up with any other 'influences'?
   a. the country you're brought up in
   b. your parents
   c. your friends
   d. the time period you live in.

3. What makes a belief 'normal' or 'strange'? Create a display board that separates 'normal' beliefs from 'strange' ones. How difficult is this?

4. Are beliefs based on evidence 'stronger' than beliefs without evidence? If something has evidence to support it, is it a belief any more?

1. In groups, choose one of the following beliefs (or come up with your own). Prepare a project or presentation on your findings. This should explain:
   a. What the belief is.
   b. Who in the world believes it and why.
   c. What evidence is behind this belief.
   d. What effects this belief has on people.
   e. How it has shaped the way of life in that country/area.

   Beliefs: life on other planets; crystal healing; alien visitors to Earth; life after death; fairies; angels; miracles; psychic powers.

2. Choose one of the beliefs above that you haven't investigated already. Now devise at least ten questions you might ask about this belief.

3. Use each of the following words to complete one sentence about beliefs: evidence; superstition; weird; reasonable; parents; upbringing; faith.

4. Someone in your class claims to have met an alien who had taken over the body of a human. Script a short dialogue that you might have with your classmate. How would you investigate their belief?

On your own

1. Use the Internet to find out about the wide range of things that people believe in. Report your findings to your class.

2. Discuss beliefs with your parents and/or friends. What beliefs do they have and why do they have them?

3. Create a piece of artwork or poetry entitled 'My beliefs'.

Kirsty is shopping at the Livingston Designer Outlet with her friend Megan. She stops at the water sculpture and reaches into her pocket, producing a pound coin. She then throws the pound coin into the water to join the many other coins there. As she does this, Megan watches curiously…

Megan: Now what did you do that for, exactly? That could have got us a happy meal.

Kirsty: For good luck.

Megan: What exactly is lucky about chucking your money away – here, give me five pounds and I'll set it on fire, dance around it and call upon the Gods of MacArthur Glen to bestow their mighty favours upon us.

Kirsty: It's good luck to throw money in a fountain … everybody does it.

Megan: Yeah, and plenty of people round here wear Adidas tracksuit trousers as formal evening clothes. Do you really think throwing money away brings you luck? I mean, who gives you the luck? Patrick the West Lothian leprechaun?

Kirsty: Now you're just being annoying.

Megan: Just trying to knock some sense into your dozy head.

[Later on, Kirsty and Megan have bought quite a lot of clothes, but in their rush to catch the bus home Kirsty didn't try on her expensive top]

Megan: I hope that top fits. It wasn't cheap, and I don't think you'll be able to return it.

Kirsty: The top will be fine … touch wood.

Megan: Touch wood? First it's magical luck-giving fairies and now it's desperate superstitions to cover you not trying on the most expensive thing you've bought today.

Kirsty: Why is it a desperate superstition?

Megan: Right, I'm going to throw myself out of the bus head first, but it'll all be ok if I utter the magic words 'touch wood' first. An army of goblins will appear from under some toadstools and save my life.

Kirsty: It's just a saying, Megan.

Megan: So is 'I've lost all my marbles and had them replaced with the brain of a hump-backed camel'.

Kirsty: Is it? What's that one all about?

Megan: Oh get a grip of yourself girl. You'll thank me for it in the end…

💬 Talking and listening

- Have you ever thrown money into a water feature (or a wishing well)? Why do people do this?
- What other things do people in your class do that might be described as 'superstitions'?
- Do you know the meaning behind any superstitions?
- Are any old-fashioned beliefs displayed in your area throughout the year? What are these all about?
- Why do many people hold onto old beliefs, even in our modern world?

Ancient and modern beliefs

Are modern beliefs any different from ancient beliefs? Have they changed over time, or just taken on new forms? Some very similar beliefs are held across cultures. For instance, many religions express the belief that death is not the end by burying people along with treasured possessions for their next life. Throughout history, most societies have attempted to keep nature happy: just as the ancient Incas of South America made human sacrifices to ensure a good harvest, so today festivals are held to celebrate the harvest or to hope for a good one (although these events are a lot less bloodthirsty nowadays!).

In Scotland, belief in river spirits and the good luck they can bring leads to the present-day practice of throwing money into water. Trees have also been worshipped as the homes of spiritual forces (so 'touch wood'). Scots used to tie cloots (strips of cloth) around the branches of trees (clootie trees) in the hope that they would bring them good luck. This practice also takes place in China and Tibet.

We might think that the modern world is all about television, the Internet and mobile phones, but it seems that some old beliefs are still around. Why is that?

Active Learning

1. Find out about a range of ancient and modern beliefs and create a display or a presentation about them. Ideally, you should look at beliefs that are held in your area and find similar beliefs that exist in other parts of the world. Here are some ideas you could investigate:
   - tree-worshipping / mistletoe / olive wreathes
   - lucky charms
   - superstitions associated with the sea, the theatre or food
   - Feng Shui
   - Up Helly Aa
   - burial practices
   - ceremonies to please natural forces
   - worship of mountains and volcanoes
   - beliefs associated with certain events in life, such as weddings or birthdays
   - beliefs associated with certain words – for example 'The Scottish Play'.

→

2. Create a wishing tree (or clootie tree) in your school. Write your wishes on strips of cloth and tie these around a tree (if you have one) or make a tree display (if you don't).

3. Try out the luck factor! Look at the website **www.quirkology.co.uk** for some scientific ideas. Get half of your class to throw a coin into a wishing well (make a small one for your class if you need to). Now compare your luck over the course of a week. Are those who threw the coin into the well luckier than those who didn't? Make charts and displays of your findings.

4. Have a discussion in class. Why have some beliefs lasted throughout history? Is it just habit? Do they bring comfort to people, or are they all childish or dangerous?

5. People sometimes express their beliefs through music or dance. Choose a piece of music (or dance) that expresses belief.

 **Progress Check**

1. For each of the following statements, say whether you agree, disagree or are not sure. Give a reason for each answer.
   b. People should be able to believe whatever they want.
   c. Some beliefs are dangerous and should be challenged.
   d. There's nothing wrong with believing in fairies and lucky charms.
   e. There are similar beliefs across the world, so there must be some truth in them.
   f. Modern beliefs are just the same as beliefs from the past.

2. Write a short report about some of the ancient and modern beliefs you might find in your local community or area.

3. Put the following statement up on a display board: 'It doesn't make sense to believe in something unless there is evidence for the belief'. Now make your own responses using post-its.

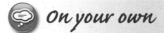 *On your own*

1. Find out about any beliefs from your area or community's past.

2. Many religious beliefs are quite like superstitions. Find one example of this and report your findings to the class. (Please be sensitive to the beliefs of others.)

3. Create a photo board about beliefs in Scotland. You could take the photos yourself or use some from the Internet.

Pupils in RME class with their teacher, having what can only be described as the eternal and yet daily debate …

Pupil 1: What's the point of RE anyway? Can we not do more maths or something?

Pupil 2: More maths, are you nuts?

Pupil 1: It's better than this.

Teacher: Right boys, calm it down a bit eh?

Pupil 1: Come on sir, you're always telling us that we should express our opinions here, aren't you?

Teacher: I'm happy to listen to your views if you'll express them a bit more calmly and think about what you're saying.

Pupil 1: Right then! We're not religious, so we don't need to learn about religion do we?

Teacher: You're not volcanoes, but you learn about them in Geography don't you?

Pupil 2: No need to be sarcastic, sir.

Teacher: Point taken. But you don't just learn things in school that fit in with the way you think about the world, do you? If that was the case you'd only be learning about football, social networking and gelling your hair…

Pupil 1: And the problem with that would be…?

Teacher: School's here to open your eyes to the world you live in. Religion is, and always has been, a big part of that world. Even if you disagree with every single word said by every follower of religion in every single time and place, you should still know what you're rejecting shouldn't you?

Pupil 2: Maybe.

Teacher: And think about how religion has influenced the world. Every culture, every country, every time, has had its beliefs, its values and its traditions – and these have had big effects on the way things are.

Pupil 1: But sir, my Dad says that religion just causes wars and conflicts, and we'd be better off without it.

Teacher: Your Dad might well be right. But wouldn't you like to make up your own mind and not just copy what your Dad believes? Would you copy how he dresses?

Pupil 1: Are you kidding – have you seen my Dad?

Teacher: Anyway, even if religion has a dark side – and even religious people would probably agree that it has – does that mean we shouldn't find out about it? Yes, people have done bad things in the name of religion, but they've done very good things too.

Pupil 2: Suppose you've got a point there. I still don't think religion's going to make any difference to me though.

Teacher: You might be right, but you won't know until you've found out a bit about it will you? Who knows, you might be surprised…

Talking and listening

- Why is religion still around in the twenty-first century?
- What is good and bad about religion?
- How might religion change in the future?
- Do you ever think about religion outside of RME?
- What evidence is there of religion in your school/community?

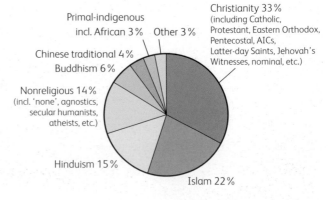

Christianity 33 % (including Catholic, Protestant, Eastern Orthodox, Pentecostal, AICs, Latter-day Saints, Jehovah's Witnesses, nominal, etc.)

Primal-indigenous incl. African 3 %

Other 3 %

Chinese traditional 4 %

Buddhism 6 %

Nonreligious 14 % (incl. 'none', agnostics, secular humanists, atheists, etc.)

Hinduism 15 %

Islam 22 %

A whole lot of religion

Wherever you go on planet Earth, you'll find religion. Religion has been responsible for lots of good things – and lots of bad things. Throughout history, people have expressed their religious beliefs through ceremonies, traditions, buildings and songs.

Religion has helped people cope with the 'big questions' we face as we go through life. It has changed history. It has led to people producing great works of art and beautiful music. It has also been responsible for some terrible things, and yet it's still around. What is it about religion that has allowed it to survive right up to the present day?

 Active Learning

1. Look at these two pictures. One is of standing stones in Scotland; the other is of Aboriginal rock art in Australia. Both are ways of expressing beliefs. On two small pieces of card, write what religious beliefs are being expressed in each of these pictures and why. There's no right or wrong answer here – just say what you think. Display these in class and discuss.

2. Choose a piece of music to go with each of these pictures. Why would you use that music? If you can, listen to the piece of music and describe your feelings about it.

3. What other religious objects and buildings are there around the world? What things do they have in common?

4. What do you think the 'big questions' in life are? What answers do you have for them?

5. Choose two or three religious artefacts (objects). For each one, prepare an information sheet about it. How does it express religious belief?

On your own

1. If you know any religious people, discuss their beliefs with them. What do they believe and why do they believe it? How do they express this belief?

2. Choose one of the 'big questions' that you identified in this section. Talk about this question with other people – perhaps even your parents. What different views do people have about it?

3. Think about your own beliefs. Why do you have these beliefs? Where did they come from? How have they changed throughout your life so far?

Progress Check

1. What does the pie chart on page 8 tell you about religious beliefs in the world today? How does this match up with your school and community? Create a questionnaire about people's religious beliefs (make sure it's anonymous) and then produce your own pie chart using your findings.

2. Use this picture to discuss the following ideas in class. Afterwards, you could write a short report on the discussion.
   b. 'When I look at the stars, I know there is a God.'
   c. 'When I look at the stars, I know that we are not alone in the Universe.'
   d. 'When I look at the stars, I know that the Universe is a wonderful place, but I don't think there's any God in it.'

3. Use the Internet to find examples of religious art and religious music. Why do you think people express their beliefs in these ways? You could design a PowerPoint presentation on this and present it to your class.

4. Choose one religion or religious belief system from the following list. Find out one thing about its beliefs, its values and its practices/traditions:
   Aboriginal peoples; Hinduism; Buddhism; Christianity; Islam; Judaism; Shinto; Bahai; Sikhism.

First there's the religions and of these the major six
Which folks around the world can choose just like a pick and mix
   There's Christian, Jews and Muslims, Sikhs and Hindus too
Not forgetting Buddhists which adds up to quite a few
These six are not so simple or so singular I'll admit
For each of them have smaller groups into which their followers split
In Islam there are Shiites who as you may quickly see
Are not the same, no not at all, as the others called Sunni
   In the Christian faith you'll find there's some who're very adamant
That they're one thing or the other, Catholic or Protestant
And even here there's more types that a Christian dude might be
Like Baptist, Methodist, C of S or even C of E
   There's high church, low church, gospel hall, and pentecostalists
Though all are sure that Jesus came and proved that God exists
There are also those which do not make the top six players' list
Like Bahai, Tao and Shinto, Rastas and Confucianist
   They're not big world religions but have many who believe
There's even some who do their thing just on midsummer's eve
Such spiritual traditions can be ancient or quite new
Pagans, Wiccans, druids, shamans – to name but very few
   And then there's some you'll only find in far-off, far-out lands
Like cargo cults such as John Frum – following our Prince Phil's commands
And groups we call indigenous – Aborigine and Sami
As well as Yanomamo, Inuit and Cherokee
   There's followers of Odin, Baal, and of Zeus still around
Though on the whole it was long ago that such beliefs were found
There's some believe in just one God, and some believe in three
And some believe in none but are religious – can that be?
   There's some who also take the mick out of all religious ways
Like Invisible Pink Unicorns, Pastafarians and X-days
Then there's those who seriously offer non-religious views
Gods, goddesses, worship, prayer and ritual they refuse
   You've only got one life to live and God does not exist
They think that humans are the best so they're called Humanist
There's beliefs we haven't mentioned yet, like Tantra and Voodoo
As well as Meher Baba, Rapa Nui and Zulu
   And also Tendai, Jodo Shu, Druze and Candomblé
And sects and groups of every kind of every holy way
And probably many others too are yet to be uncovered
In far-off lands or just next door to you they'll be discovered
   So when your neighbour starts to wear a silky yellow handkerchief
Watch out cos it just might be a whole new strange belief …

💬 *Talking and listening*

- Why are there so many varieties of belief in the world?
- Can all these beliefs be 'true'?
- Does it matter what beliefs you have?
- Do you know of any followers of any of these beliefs?
- Do some beliefs make more sense than others?

A world of beliefs

Some beliefs are religious and some are not. The six major religions in the world have many followers, but does that make them any more important (or real)? Religions agree about lots of things, but they also disagree strongly about others. Does that make some right and some wrong, or all right or all wrong? There are also many 'smaller' religions, some of which were formed out of the 'big six'. Some spiritual traditions and ways of life, such as those of the Arctic Inuit, have been around for longer than the six major world religions. There are also beliefs that are the opposite of religion (such as Humanism) and others that poke fun at religion (such as the Church of the Flying Spaghetti Monster). But it looks like beliefs are here to stay – in all sorts of forms. What are your beliefs? Where did they come from?

 *Active Learning*

1. In groups, choose one of the six major world religions or Humanism. Create a short illustrated factfile about the belief (or viewpoint) you have chosen. This should cover:
   a. its main ideas
   b. a little history
   c. important figures
   d. an image that represents the belief/viewpoint.

2. On a world map, mark where you would find some of the beliefs mentioned in the poem. (Don't mark world religions or Humanism.) You could do this as an interactive ICT project by creating pop-ups that appear when you hover the mouse over a particular country. Each pop-up could have an image and a short piece of information about the belief.

3. Home and away: choose two of the beliefs or belief systems in the poem (not one of the world religions or Humanism). One should be a belief that you might find in your community or in Scotland; the other should be one that you wouldn't find in Scotland. Find out about these beliefs and find an image that represents each one.

4. Past and present: create a display showing beliefs that are still present in the world and those that are mostly from the past. This display could be very artistic, and it could be a timeline of beliefs from around your class.

5. Choose three religions. Find three things that they agree about and three things that they disagree about.

1. Copy and complete the following table, including all the beliefs and belief systems mentioned in the poem and any others you have found during your research.

Name of belief/ belief system	Is this religious or non-religious?	Is this linked to only one place or group of people?	Is this present in the world today?	Is this present in Scotland today?

2. Take this starter sentence around your class and ask as many people as you can to complete it. Now explain what you think your class is saying in response to it. 'There are loads of beliefs in the world today, of many different kinds. I think this…'

3. Have a class discussion and note down some of the views you hear. This should be based on the following statement: 'it doesn't matter what you believe, as long as you believe in something'.

4. Write your own poem about beliefs around the world. See how many religions, beliefs or belief systems you can get into this poem. Perhaps you could do this as a class, with groups taking a verse each.

On your own

1. Have a look at the BBC web page on religions at **www.bbc.co.uk/religion/religions/** or go to **www.religionfacts.com/**. Choose one religion or belief system that you haven't covered in any way during your work in this section. Write down what you find out.

2. What beliefs are present in your community (or family)? Do some research and be prepared to report your findings.

3. When people are talking about beliefs, they sometimes use the word 'spirituality'. Do an Internet search on this word and write about what you discover.

[*To the tune of 'Old Macdonald had a farm'*]

Old Macdonald just assumed,
ee-i-ee-i-oh
He had no facts but he
presumed, ee-i-ee-i-oh
With no evidence here, no
evidence there, he even believed
that he had hair
Old Macdonald just assumed,
ee-i-ee-i-oh

Old Macdonald lived in trust,
ee-i-ee-i-oh
'Til his lucky charm got bust,
ee-i-ee-i-oh
Horse shoes here, rabbit's foot
there, not stepping on the cracks
or passing on the stair
Old Macdonald lived in trust,
ee-i-ee-i-oh

Old Macdonald's faith held
strong, ee-i-ee-i-oh
Though his beliefs were very
wrong, ee-i-ee-i-oh
The proof was here, the proof
was there, but Old Macdonald
didn't care
Old Macdonald's faith held
strong, ee-i-ee-i-oh

Old Macdonald tried to reason,
ee-i-ee-i-oh
That winter was the warmest
season, ee-i-ee-i-oh
The snow was here, the ice was
there, though it was toasty he
would swear
Old Macdonald tried to reason,
ee-i-ee-i-oh

Old Macdonald did not doubt,
ee-i-ee-i-oh
But didn't bother to find out,
ee-i-ee-i-oh
If climbing high, then trying to
fly, would surely mean that he
would die
Old Macdonald did not doubt,
ee-i-ee-i-oh

[*Sadly and slowly*]

Now Old Macdonald's passed
away, ee-i-ee-i-oh
He lived his life in his own way,
ee-i-ee-i-oh
Is there a Heaven or an afterlife,
or is there a Hell full of grief and
strife
Old Macdonald's passed away,
ee-i-ee-i-oh

Old Macdonald's very frustrated,
ee-i-ee-i-oh
He might have been
reincarnated, ee-i-ee-i-oh
He may be someone's brand
new pet, or be a llama in Tibet
Old Macdonald's very frustrated,
ee-i-ee-i-oh

What have we learned from this
tale of woe, ee-i-ee-i-oh
That you may believe but you do
not know, ee-i-ee-i-oh
If faith and trust, mean that you
must, live on forever or turn to
dust
Old Macdonald's gone away,
where-we-do-not-know

Ah-ah-men

Talking and listening

- Do you need evidence before you believe in something?
- Do you have any beliefs that are based on pure trust?
- What do you believe happens after death? Why do you believe this?
- Is there always a difference between believing something and knowing something?
- Does it matter what a person believes?

Believe it or not

Faith means believing without needing evidence to support your belief. In fact, faith sometimes means believing things even when the evidence goes against you. Most religious beliefs are based on faith, but some non-religious beliefs also have bits of 'faith' in them.

We all act on trust sometimes. In fact, have a look at a ten-pound note. This little bit of paper isn't worth much on its own – but you trust that when you hand it over in a shop then the person will give you ten pounds' worth of products for it. In today's world, belief can be split into two: beliefs that are supported by evidence and beliefs that need no evidence. Is belief a part of your life? Do you believe things only where there's evidence?

Active Learning

1. Write up the following topics on a display board. Now add post-its with your anonymous beliefs about each topic.
   - Is there life after death?
   - Do souls exist?
   - Is there a God?
   - Should animals be treated the same way as humans?
   - Why do people suffer?
   - Does life have a meaning?
   - How did the Universe begin?
   - Is there a Loch Ness monster?

2. If you can, invite someone to talk to your class about his or her beliefs. Devise some questions and make your own notes about the things they say. You could video your interviews with this person and save them for future classes. Alternatively, have a look on the Internet for interviews with people who have beliefs. Try **www.retoday.org.uk/downloads.htm**.

3. Design a poster, 'One Scotland, Many Beliefs', which celebrates the different beliefs that exist in our country.

4. Discuss the following issues:
   a. Are there any beliefs that should be banned?
   b. Should children be told what to believe by anyone?
   c. Is it right for parents to expect their children to accept their beliefs?
   d. At what age should children make up their own minds about what they believe?
   e. Does it matter what you believe?

5. Every time you get in an aeroplane, you trust the pilots with your life. What other things do you do based on trust?

1. Find definitions for the following words and write them in your jotter. You could use a dictionary, a thesaurus or an Internet search:
    - faith; reason; trust; evidence; superstition; rational; irrational; logical; illogical; mystery; certainty.

2. Find out about someone whose beliefs affected their life. Try to get a picture of the person; explain what their beliefs are and how these beliefs helped them or caused them problems. The person doesn't have to be famous – it could be someone in your community or someone you know. Or it could be a figure from history or someone from the world of sport, music or entertainment.

3. Look back through this unit on Beliefs and answer the following questions for yourself:
    a. What have I learned about my beliefs?
    b. What have I learned about the beliefs of others?
    c. What have I learned about where beliefs come from and how they develop?
    d. What questions do I still have about beliefs?
    e. What other things would I like to find out about beliefs?
    f. Have any of my beliefs been changed or challenged in this unit?
    g. Do I have a better understanding of beliefs now than before I started this unit?
    h. What things have I been good at doing throughout this unit?
    i. What would I still like to improve about my learning in future units?

On your own

1. Devise a short test about what you have learned in this unit. It could be a multiple-choice or short-answer test. Make sure there are not just factual questions but questions about how people have developed their understanding of the topic of beliefs.

2. Go to **www.retoday.org.uk/downloads.htm** and read an interview with a young religious person or a 'citizen of faith'.

2

Exploring Buddhism

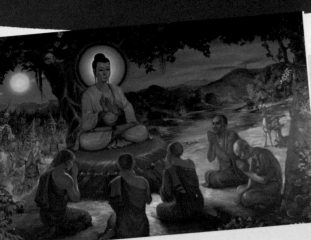

Rab and Donnie are two ordinary men from Glasgow, but they often have discussions about things that are definitely not ordinary. Rab has been to the garden centre and bought himself a nice new little statue for his garden. He's about to show it to Donnie…

Donnie: So whit did ye buy? Some pansies fur yer herbaceous border? A roller fur yer carpet-like lawn?

Rab: I bought a Buddha.

Donnie: Ye bought a Buddha. Ye'll no be too offended if I ask ye why, will ye?

Rab: Naw … it's nice.

Donnie: Nice … so whit exactly dae ye ken aboot this Buddha, then?

Rab: He was a god guy.

Donnie: So ye want to fill yer garden wi' gods and goddesses then, dae ye? Whit aboot a life-size statue o' Jesus and Mary as well? And while ye're at it, why no add a big Hindu god here and there and … whit aboot a ten-foot totem pole? Or even better, how's aboot a twenty-foot-high wicker man?

Rab: Do ye no think that would be a wee bit over the top Donnie?

Donnie: I dinnae suppose anybody would be too surprised at whit they found in yer garden Rab. But anyway, ye cannae just go an buy a Buddha cos ye like it – it's no like that.

Rab: So why does the garden centre sell them, then?

Donnie: Maybe cos they want tae spread universal peace and joy and fill the world wi' cosmic harmony? Or maybe they just want tae make money through sellin' holy figures tae numpties like you.

Rab: So should I take it back, then?

Donnie: Up tae you Rab … but dae ye no think it's a wee bit strange that people have these things in their gardens and hooses? After all, there's no that many Buddhists floatin' aboot around here.

Rab: I'm a bit confused noo.

Donnie: That'll be ye back tae yer comfort zone then Rab. Anyway Rab, come tae think of it, there's a more important problem wi' this whole idea … ye've no got a garden. Ye live on the fourteenth floor o' a skyscraper overlookin' the M8…

Talking and listening

- Have you seen any statues of Buddha in shops or garden centres? Do you have any at home, or know anyone who does?
- Does it make sense to have a statue of a religious figure if you don't follow that religion?
- Does anyone in your class have any religious objects in their home or garden? Why do they have these?
- Sometimes, religious figures find their way onto t-shirts or get turned into objects of fun. What do you think about that?
- Some people like having Buddha statues because they make them 'feel calm'. What do you think about that?

The Buddha

Siddartha Gautama was a rich prince who lived in a palace in northern India long ago. He had a fabulous life of pleasure, with his every wish granted. His father had been told that Siddartha would become a holy man if he ever saw what life was really like, so he tried to shield Siddartha from everything bad. However, one day Siddartha escaped from the palace and went to the local village. Here he saw four sights: an old man, a sick man, a dead body and a holy man. He decided to leave the palace, and left his wife and son behind. He tried in various ways to work out the meaning of life, like starving himself and partying like mad. But nothing worked, and eventually he decided to sit and meditate until he understood the meaning of life. When this happened, he became the enlightened one, or the Buddha. He spent the rest of his life teaching others about what he had discovered. He never claimed to be a god, but the religion of Buddhism developed following his teachings. Buddhists can now be found all over the world.

Active Learning

1. Retell the story of the Buddha's visit to the village and how this changed his life. You could do this as a drama, a cartoon, a presentation or a poem, or you could write a diary from the point of view of Siddartha Gautama. Try not to just tell the story, but instead express how Siddartha might have felt about what he was seeing and experiencing, and how this was changing his view of the world.

2. Find out about the different kinds of Buddha statue, either by looking online or by borrowing them from pupils or teachers. You could even set up an exhibition of Buddhas in your class. You'll find that the Buddha is represented in many different ways. Sometimes he's standing, lying or sitting and his hands are often making particular signs. What do these all mean?

3. When the Buddha was meditating under the Bodhi tree, he was tempted by the demon Mara. Create a piece of artwork that illustrates the idea that the Buddha was torn between doing what was right and what was wrong in his life. He could have been selfish or selfless. How might you illustrate this?

4. When the Buddha died, Buddhism spread around the world. But it also split up into different groups and 'schools'. Find out about the major schools of Buddhism. You could use photos of different kinds of Buddhism and create a wall display for your class.

5. Using some modelling clay or plasticine, make your own Buddha statues.

1. Here are some different views about having a statue of the Buddha in your home or garden (if you're not a Buddhist). For each one, explain whether you agree or disagree and why.
   a. There's nothing wrong with having a Buddha statue in your home or garden.
   b. Statues of religious figures are not decorations, they are holy objects.
   c. Having a Buddha statue if you are not a Buddhist is offensive to Buddhists.

2. Sit in a circle. After the first line below, each person should add one sentence to the story of the Buddha's life from rich young prince to holy man. Try to put as much detail into the story as you can. 'There once was a rich ruler who had a son…'

3. Find out what is meant by a mudra. What different kinds of mudra are there and what do they mean? You could create an illustrated information sheet on this using photos of your own hands.

4. Imagine you had been able to meet the Buddha after his enlightenment. What questions would you have asked him about his life?

![icon] On your own

1. Visit **www.buddhanet.net/audio.htm**. Here you can listen to Buddhist chanting, speeches and songs (you can even download them as MP3s!).

2. Visit **www.buddhanet.net/mag_kids.htm**, where you can make your own Buddha image by dragging and dropping the parts of the picture.

3. Look up the story of Kisagotami on the Internet. Be ready to present the story to your class and explain what it tells us about the Buddha's teaching.

Reader 1: [*Reads gloomily and a little spookily*]
Hi, my name is Suffering and I am all around
Wherever there is doom and gloom – and sadness – I'll be found
When you're ill or miserable or you fell and skint your knee
Somewhere I'll be lurking – but not that you can see
(Just as I was, so long ago for Kis-a-go-ta-mi)
When there are wars and famines, fires, crashes, death and pain
Or maybe just a rotten day of thunder, winds and rain
I'm not just in the big things though, like when you're very sick
I could just be an irritant that's getting on your wick
Some niggly small annoying thing that chips away at you
Like when your hols are ending and you're starting to feel blue
So when your life is gloomy or with guilt you are aflame
Don't forget it's all my fault – and Dukkha is my name

Reader 2: [*Reads in a cheesy way*]
And then there's me, my name's Desire and I may live in you
Like when you simply have to have the latest thing that's new
Even if the old one's good and working pretty well
You chuck it out or smash it up or tell your mum it fell
So you can have the latest one or simply something better
A new mobile, some hot new shoes, or a different type of sweater
It doesn't matter what it is, it's just what you desire
A PS twelve, 3D TV or a force-ten-gale hair dryer
When you are being selfish and you're filled with want and greed
You'll find me there, for these are things on which I feast and feed
I'm never satisfied you see, I'm always wanting more
My name is Tanha, and you'll find I'm always at your door

Reader 3: [*Reads normally*]
So is there no way to avoid this misery and woe?
I bet you hope the answer isn't just a simple no
There is a way to end Dukkha, to banish it from sight
You need to stop desiring, which will give Dukkha a fright
You have to give up selfishness and put
an end to
greed
Stop
wanting
things
you
cannot
have or
thinking
that you
need

To have more stuff, more fame, more joy, more days upon the beach
You have to stop desiring, get away from Tanha's reach
To stop desire is Nirodha – that's me, I'm on your side
Detach yourself from worldly wants – that's what you must decide
Have no desire, stop wanting things for then you surely may
Be free from Dukkha's gloomy grip through following the Middle Way

Reader 4: [*Brightly*]
That Middle Way is me my friend, and from Dukkha's clutch I save
I'll help you fight off Tanha so that you'll no longer crave
The things that never last at all – that are just feeble, fleeting
Or end up with you miserable or maybe even greeting
My name is Magga and I can help you conquer Dukkha's wrath
By showing you the magic way, the noble Eightfold Path

💬 Talking and listening

- What examples of suffering are there in the world today?
- What kinds of things cause this suffering?
- What things do people desire?
- Are you ever greedy? How does this make you feel? What does it mean for other people?
- Why do people always seem to want the latest fashion or latest gadget? When people get it, are they always happy?

⚙️ Active Learning

1. Create a class display: 'Suffering in the World'. Use magazine images and newspaper articles. Try to show not only 'big and serious' examples of suffering like wars, but 'little' examples of suffering such as feeling a bit sad about something.

2. Write a poem or create a piece of artwork entitled 'What People Want'. Here are some ideas for you to think about: winning the lottery; having the latest gadgets; being famous; being popular; becoming a top footballer, and so on…

3. Sometimes people get tied to things and don't even realise it. Imagine you could start a completely new life tomorrow and change anything you want about your life. What things would you get rid of? What would you replace them with? How do you think you could make yourself more contented? Write a letter to yourself saying how you could detach yourself from the things that are tying you to the world.

4. Have a look through some magazines appropriate for people of your age. Do they encourage you to want things? How do they do this? Are the things they encourage you to want meaningful things? Do they make life better? Prepare a short talk or presentation on this for your class.

5. Many stories are based on the idea of wishes being granted and everything ending happily ever after. What happens after the main character gets what they want, though? Do they remain happy for long? Choose a story you know and write a 'What happened next?' section. Did getting the things they wanted really satisfy them?

The Four Noble Truths

The Buddha taught that the way to escape the endless suffering of life was to stop craving things or desiring things. He said that this craving tied you to the world like chains, and that the only way to be truly contented is to detach yourself from the things of the world. Like a mouse running in a wheel, we keep chasing new things and new experiences because we hope they will satisfy us – but they never do. The only way to be truly happy is to escape this wheel. Buddhists call this attaining Nibbana, which is where you stop all desire and so stop all suffering. The way to do this is by following the Eightfold Path.

1. In groups, discuss and write answers to the following questions:
   a. Is life really full of suffering?
   b. Is the idea that 'life is full of suffering' a miserable, negative way to look at the world?
   c. Is there anything wrong with wanting things?
   d. Is it possible to stop desiring things?

2. Make a top ten of things that cause suffering in the world.

3. How does greed cause suffering? Discuss this question in groups, thinking about it in relation to:
   a. you
   b. your school
   c. your local community
   d. Scotland
   e. the world.

4. Write one question you would ask of Dukkha, Tanha, Nirodha and Magga. What answer might they give?

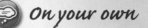 **On your own**

1. Carry out a survey among people your age. What do they want from life? Prepare a short report on your findings. You could compare this with a survey carried out on adults or older children. Will people your age in other parts of the world want the same things?

2. Find out about Buddhist beliefs about Nibbana. What is it and how do you get it?

3. Here is a piece of artwork illustrating Buddhist beliefs about the wheel of existence, which you must escape to attain Nibbana. Discuss this image with others. What does it tell you about Buddhist beliefs?

8 The Eightfold Path

[A group of eight cheerleaders and their leader are just about to practise a new routine…]

Leader: [Bright and bubbly] Give me a B! **All:** [Shout loudly] B!
Leader: Give me an A! **All:** A!
Leader: Give me an S! **All:** S!
Leader: Give me a C! **All:** C!
Leader: Give me an L! **All:** L!
Leader: Give me an E! **All:** E!
Leader: Give me an M! **All:** M!
Leader: Give me an M! **All:** M!
Leader: Put them all together, and
      what have you got?! **All:** BASCLEMM!!!!!

[All mutter to each other at the same time … 'Basclemm?', 'What's all that about?',
'Did we get that right?']

Cheerleader 1: Eh … coach … what's Basclemm?
Leader: The Noble Eightfold Path of Buddhism, of course.
Cheerleader 1: Which is?
Leader: The meaning of life – how you avoid suffering and escape the wheel of life and attain Nibbana …
Cheerleader 2: You feeling ok, coach? Pressure of competition getting to you a bit?
Leader: No, I just thought we'd do something different for a change.
Cheerleader 3: Well, maybe if you explained it to us …

The Eightfold Path: 'BASCLEMM'

This was the last of the Four Noble Truths. It was the Buddha's guide to living a good life, escaping suffering and finding true peace.

1. Right **B**eliefs: you can follow the teaching of Buddha and realise that the trouble with life is Dukkha caused by Tanha. This way of thinking will help you make sense of life.

2. Right **A**ctions: there's no point in believing the right things if you don't put your beliefs into action. You should act towards others in the right way.

3. Right **S**peech: you should use your words to build people up, not knock them down. What you say reflects what you think and the kind of person you are.

4. Right **C**onduct: you should act correctly in everything you do – no matter how small it seems. For example, as a student, you should conduct yourself well in school at all times – not because of the rules, but because it's right.

5. Right **L**ivelihood: your work should not harm any other living thing. So choose a job that's helpful, not harmful.

6. Right **E**ffort: you need to work at it – whatever it is. This might be little things or your whole approach to life

7. Right **M**indfulness: this is about how you see things. It's about noticing the little things in life, but also seeing them for what they are. For example, will the things you want in life really make you happy?

8. Right **M**editation: meditation is about clearing your mind of all the clutter that's in it, so that you can think clearly and see things for what they are.

Talking and listening

- What do you think are the 'right' beliefs?
- Is it ok to do whatever you want in life?
- Can words harm? Should some words be avoided?
- How do you know when you're doing wrong?
- Are some jobs more harmful or helpful than others?
- Do you think people sometimes give up too easily?
- Are you realistic about the kind of person you are and the kinds of things you can and can't do?
- How easy is it to empty your mind and clear your head?

Active Learning

1. Design your own illustrated poster on the Eightfold Path.

2. For each of the parts of the Eightfold Path that are 'right', write down what their opposite might be – what would be 'wrong'?

3. Write out a number of words and phrases. Now stick them on a board under the headings 'Right Speech' or 'Wrong Speech'. What makes words right or wrong?

4. Draw up a list of jobs that might be 'right' and 'wrong' livelihoods. Which jobs help others? Which jobs might harm others? Are there any jobs that might have a bit of both in them?

5. Practise right mindfulness. Set up a table with a number of everyday objects – things that you are very familiar with, such as rocks, pencils, spoons and so on. Now look at them again. Try to imagine that you are looking at them for the first time. Now describe them in as much detail as you can – not only how they look but what they do. See how many of your five senses you can use in describing these familiar objects.

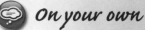

Progress Check

1. Discuss these opposing statements in class. What does each one mean? Which ones do you agree with and why?

There's no such thing as a right belief	When your beliefs are wrong, everything's wrong
It's the thought that counts – the actions don't matter	Actions speak louder than words
Sticks and stones may break my bones, but names will never hurt me	Verbal bullying is as bad as any other kind
It ain't what you do, it's the way that you do it	Something is only wrong when it leads to wrong actions
A Buddhist could never be a butcher	Being a school teacher is an example of a right livelihood
People just take the easy way out these days	You have not failed unless you failed to try
People sometimes can't see the wood for the trees	Take things as they are, you'll only get confused if you try to think about them too much
Meditation is a pointless waste of time – you'd be better doing something useful	Everyone's mind is too busy nowadays

2. Which parts of the Eightfold Path do you think you already follow in your life? Would your life be better if you followed all of these teachings? What would be the easiest ones for you to follow? What would be the hardest ones?

3. Keep a mindfulness diary for a week. In this diary, try to write down things that you wouldn't usually notice. See the detail and try to see things as they are. What things do you notice that you didn't before? What effect does this have on you? Are you calmer? More aware?

4. Scottish people are sometimes not very good at being positive about themselves, or others. Create a positive board in your class. On this, you should only write positive comments about anything you like. You could use the following categories:
   a. yourself
   b. others in your class/school
   c. your school and its teachers
   d. your community
   e. Scotland.

On your own

1. Sometimes the Eightfold Path is phrased a little differently. Look it up on the Internet and write out the different words for each of the eight parts that you find.

2. Have a look through some newspapers or magazines. See if you can find examples of things that are linked to the Eightfold Path (for example, you might find examples of people using words to harm or build people up).

3. Carry out a survey among your classmates and family. Which parts of the Eightfold Path do they follow and which do they not follow? You might need to explain each one to them first.

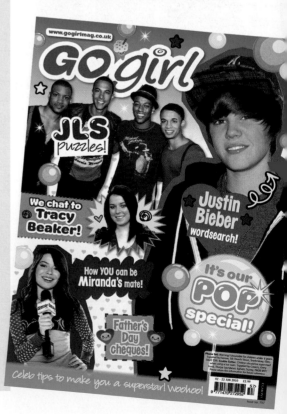

Tim, a first-year pupil, walks into a classroom to discover his classmate Tom sitting on the floor cross-legged, with his arms by his side and fingers pointed. Tom seems to be humming to himself with his eyes closed, and Tim has no idea what Tom's doing…

Tim: Earth calling Tom, come in Tom, anyone in Tom? *[Knocks Tom on the head like he's knocking a door. Tom opens his eyes slowly]*

Tom: Yes, and why are you disturbing my meditative spiritual moment?

Tim: What on Earth were you up to – you looked like you were communicating with aliens.

Tom: No, just communicating with my inner self.

Tim: Oh right, silly me, I get it. Ok, no I don't. What were you up to exactly?

Tom: Meditating. I would have thought that was pretty obvious.

Tim: Meditating? When did you get into that?

Tom: We went on a trip to Samye Ling last week – I thought it was quite cool so I've been trying it out all week.

Tim: Samye Ling?

Tom: It's a Buddhist temple down in Dumfries. It's brilliant – it's got giant Buddhas and monks and stupas and everything.

Tim: So what's this meditation for?

Tom: Well first it clears your mind – vacuums out all the dust and grunge hanging about in there. Then, when it's all clear and peaceful, you can rearrange the furniture and put things where you want them.

Tim: You make it sound like redecorating the inside of your head.

Tom: It is like that I suppose. It helps you to see things more clearly.

Tim: Like … what do you want to see?

Tom: Well, sometimes we think the world is one way when it's actually not like that at all. I'm trying to make sense of the world, the meaning of it all.

Tim: And you think sitting cross-legged in your RME class might help you to do that?

Tom: Don't see why not.

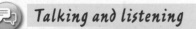

Talking and listening

- What were the last five thoughts (in a row) that went through your head?
- Do you agree that your mind is busy and always full of stuff?
- Do you find it easy to sit in silence and empty your mind, or is it difficult?
- Where (or when) do you find it easiest to be calm, quiet and peaceful?
- Do you think it is possible to work out the meaning of life by just sitting in your RME classroom? If not, what would be the best way to find it out?

Meditation

Buddhists believe that it is not enough just to study their religion. They think that you can only really understand it by practising it through meditation. Meditation is a way of calming yourself and clearing your mind of all the clutter that's lying around in there. It is also a way of controlling the mind – this is important because Buddhists think a lot of our problems come because we are not in control of our minds. It is also a way to see yourself and other things as they really are, instead of as they appear to be. Once you can do this, you are off on the journey towards enlightenment – just like the Buddha. Meditation can be done by chanting a mantra – a special holy saying – or by being completely silent. You can meditate on an image of the Buddha, or an everyday object, or a Buddhist teaching and so on. Buddhists think you should find the kind of meditation that suits you best and stick with it. Meditation puts you in touch with yourself.

Active Learning

1. You could try some meditating, but only with your teacher's guidance and only if he or she is comfortable doing so. Ideally you should get a Buddhist to take you through some simple meditation. Or you could find a quiet place and sit in silence for a while. You will find that your mind is all over the place and that you think about one thing after another. Try not to block things out of your mind, but instead see the thoughts coming and going in your mind. You could sit and look at an everyday object, like a leaf. Try to focus only on the object and see it in all its detail – every shade of colour, every texture, every subtle thing that you would usually miss.

2. If you manage to try some meditation, write about your experience. What did you like about it? What did you not like? Did you enjoy the feeling of calm? Did you think it was a waste of time?

3. Buddhists might use certain things to help them during meditation. Find out about each one of the following. How is it used to help in meditation?
   a. singing bowl
   b. bell
   c. Buddha image
   d. incense
   e. chanting mantras
   f. prayer wheels.

4. Zen Buddhism uses koans to help meditation. These are short sayings that at first don't appear to make any sense. The idea is that you meditate on them and then your normal thinking processes are replaced by a more enlightened kind of thinking. Here is one example: 'Two hands clapping make a sound. What is the sound made by one hand clapping?' Think about this saying for a while and then discuss in class – does it make any sense? Does it matter if it makes any sense? You can find some more koans at www.ashidakim.com/zenkoans/zenindex.html.

5. Find out about the different body positions used during meditation as well as the different hand shapes (try www.wildmind.org/posture/intro for starters). Design an informative poster about your findings.

Progress Check

1. Discuss these two opposing statements in class and note down any interesting ideas that are expressed:
   a. Meditation is a good way to clear your mind and help you understand yourself.
   b. Meditation is just sitting around doing nothing and is a complete waste of time.

2. Practise mindfulness. Look at an object you see every day, and now describe it in as much detail as you can.

3. Given what you now know about Buddhism, do you think a Buddhist should meditate to make themselves *feel better*? Discuss in class.

4. Meditation can be about doing anything in a mindful way. What ordinary actions could you do in a meditative way?

5. Buddhists often use meditation to send out good thoughts to others. What problems in the world might benefit from this? Is this even possible?

On your own

1. Many websites offer examples of meditation. You can even download podcasts of meditation, chanting, koans and so on. Go to www.how-to-meditate.org/, or watch some Buddhist meditation on YouTube at www.youtube.com/watch?v=Rd7a9Ur2x0o and report back to your class. Remember, you should really only do meditation with an experienced guide so don't try it yourself!

2. Buddhists often use a Buddha statue to help them focus during meditation. These statues come in many shapes and forms. Have a look at Google Images for Buddha statues and choose one that appeals to you. Why do you like it?

3. Buddhists believe that meditation helps you to see yourself as you really are. Do you think you can see yourself as you really are?

Here are three pieces of Buddhist art. Study each one very carefully for at least three minutes. You should do this in complete silence.

Expressing Buddhism through art

Art is about making sense of the world and expressing what matters to you. Artists choose the subject of their art very carefully and they choose their materials equally carefully. Religious art often has an added feature: the artist is trying to express their beliefs through their art, but also wants to honour its subject. The Buddhist art you looked at was:

- A thanka: this is a very ornate painting of Buddha (or Boddhisattva) figures.
  The painting may include symbols and images that say something about the personal qualities of the Buddha or Boddhisattva figure.
- A mandala: these shapes help Buddhists focus during meditation. They are sometimes made of coloured sand and then destroyed.
- A Buddha statue: these may show a point in the life of the Buddha or, like the thanka, describe qualities of Buddhas or Boddhisattvas.

Buddhists take great care when creating art linked to their faith. It is a way of expressing what matters to them and making sense of their lives. How do you express what matters to you?

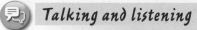 Talking and listening

- Describe each of the three pieces of art in as much detail as you can (without looking at them again).
- Why do you think they were made, and who might have made them?
- How long do you think each one took to make?
- What reasons were behind the choice of colours or the style of the art?
- How can you tell that a great deal of care went into the making of each one?
- How do these pieces of art make you feel?

Active Learning

1. Make your own piece of Buddhist art. It could be a drawing or painting, or a model, or a mandala – perhaps even one made of coloured sand. Plan your art carefully and think about the size it will be, where it will be displayed and what its purpose is. You might have to look on the Internet for ideas. It is also perfectly ok to copy artwork. Many Buddhist pieces of art are copies of images and statues that have been handed down for thousands of years. Perhaps you could have an exhibition of your work once it has been completed.

2. Think about the thing or things that matter to you most in your life. Create a piece of artwork about the most important things in your life.

3. Find out about one piece of Buddhist art and create a short factsheet about it. Who made it? Why? Where is it? What is it trying to express?

4. The sand mandalas are linked to an important Buddhist belief called anicca. This is the idea that everything is impermanent. Find out more about this Buddhist belief and explain how the creation and destruction of the sand mandalas express this idea.

5. Some types of Buddhism, such as Zen Buddhism, have no real art as part of their worship. Find out why this is and discuss whether you think this is a good idea or not.

1. Here are two opposing viewpoints about Buddhist art (and religious art in general). Discuss each one and decide what you think about them. What are the reasons behind your thinking?
   a. It is right for Buddhists to spend a lot of time, energy and money creating great pieces of religious art.
   b. Buddhists should not spend their time, energy and money creating pieces of religious art – they should do something more worthwhile instead.

2. Get hold of a Buddha image. Add notes around the image explaining what each part of the image represents.

3. Buddhists sometimes use their art as a form of meditation. In what way(s) might creating any piece of artwork be a kind of meditation? Discuss in class and note down the views expressed.

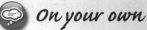

1. If you can get to a museum with religious objects (or even a shop), visit it and make a note of the variety of pieces of Buddhist art there are in existence.

2. Do a search on Google Images for pieces of Buddhist art. See if you can find one that you really like. Explain why you have chosen it.

3. Have a look at some of the artwork in your Art department at school. What ideas, feelings or beliefs is the artwork trying to express? You could discuss this with your Art teacher too.

3

Human rights

Reader 1: [*A very happy girl*] I love clothes! I love all kinds of clothes! They don't need to cost much or have big designer labels – as long as they look good on me. I have hundreds of tops, hundreds of dresses… and let's not even think about how many pairs of shoes I've got…

Reader 2: [*A very unhappy girl*] I make clothes. The clothes I make get sold in far-away countries that I'll never see. The people who buy them are richer than I could be even in my wildest dreams. I work very hard. They beat me if I don't work hard enough, and if they don't think my work is good enough they don't pay me for that day. They still sell the clothes I made, though. The people who buy them know nothing about me. I suppose they like it better that way.

Reader 3: [*A very happy boy*] I love football, and I've just got a new ball. It's quality. When I play with this it'll turn me into a star. It's sleek and smooth and shiny and new – almost seems a shame to kick it. But kick it I will…

Reader 4: [*A very unhappy boy*] I love football, but I have no time to play it. I'm too busy making… footballs. Because I've got small fingers I'm good at sewing the balls up. It really does hurt sometimes, but I've just got to get on with it. If I don't make enough balls in a day then they'll hit me or kick me out. I need what little money they usually pay me. How else would I survive?

Reader 5: [*A very happy boy*] How's this for a phone, then? Does everything. Apps for anything you can imagine. Only a couple of hundred quid, and millions of free texts. I could make a movie on this phone. I could probably contact another planet on this phone.

Reader 6: [*A very unhappy boy*] I spend my day in a mine – it's like Hell on Earth. It's hot and damp, and it smells. They say that we breathe in demons down here and that's why so many of us miners go mad. I sometimes get bad headaches – but no wonder when I'm choking on the dusty air and peering in what little light there is. I load the rocks on the carts. They sparkle. They say that the sparkling bits are what they really want. They use it in electronic things like mobile phones.

🗨 Talking and listening

- What are your favourite things?
- Think through the things you own. How much do you know about where those things came from? How could you find out where they came from?
- When you buy something, how important are the following things: the cost of the item; how it looks; how trendy it is; what other people might think of it; the quality of the item?
- Would you be prepared to pay more for something if you knew that doing so would help make the producer's life better? How much extra would you be prepared to pay? Five per cent, ten per cent, fifty per cent?

Child slavery

Maybe you thought slaves were something from the past. Think again. In today's world many children still work in dirty, dangerous and exhausting jobs. They work to pay off money owed by their parents, or sometimes their parents sell them and their new owners make them work hard. In most countries there are laws to prevent this, but sometimes these laws are just ignored. Some children work because they have to: perhaps they have been thrown out by their parents, or their parents are in prison or dead. These children will do almost any kind of work to make a little money in order to survive. Such children hardly ever get to play or learn – or do the things that a normal child can do. So the next time you say that you have nothing to do, remember that some children in the world have more to do than they can ever cope with. Remember, too, that the last cheap thing you bought might only have been cheap because it was produced by a child slave.

Active Learning

1. Make a list of the things you own. Work out how much each thing is worth. For each item, explain where you bought it and how much you know about how it was produced.

2. Find out about abuses of children's rights around the world. On a world map, mark as many places as you can where children work. Describe what is done by the children and make some comment about the conditions the children might experience. You could look at www.unicef.org, www.antislavery.org and www.stopchildlabour.net to help you.

3. In recent years, many pop stars and bands have written songs and performed at concerts to get people thinking about important issues. Write your own song to make people more aware of child labour issues around the world. You could set this to any tune you like – or, of course, write your own.

4. Barcelona Football Club pays a children's charity a large sum of money to use its logo on their shirts. What other things could sport / music / business / individuals do to help make children's lives better?

5. What special rights should children have? Draw up your own charter of children's rights and compare it with the UN Declaration on the Rights of the Child at www.un.org/cyberschoolbus/humanrights/resources/plainchild.asp.

1. What rights do you think you have? What rights should people your age have? Are your rights being granted? What changes could there be in your school, community or country that would improve your rights?

2. Here are two statements about the rights of a child labourer. For each one, set out the possible arguments that might support it. You could debate this in class:
   'Children should never have to work until they are adults.'
   'Children should be allowed to work – they are people just like everyone else.'

3. Now that you have learned more about the rights of children, as well as the problems facing child labourers in today's world, write out ten things that you could do to help stop child labour and child slavery.

4. Design and make a short information leaflet about why child slavery should be stopped.

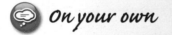 *On your own*

1. Find out about the plight of one child or situation where children are used as slaves or forced labour and prepare a short report for your class about this.

2. Use one of the photos in this section to write a piece of poetry, drama or imaginative writing that matches the photo.

3. 'Every child matters'. Explain your own views on this statement after discussing with others and suggest how you could make this idea become a reality in the world today.

Reader

1: Boring, boring, BORING. Man I really hate school. Here at Auchertuchty Academy all we ever do is the same old stuff. Copy this, read this, draw this picture, discuss this, blah blah. Mind you, it's worse when the teacher tries to use technology –drag this picture into the right box to match up with the answer, copy notes from PowerPoint. And then we get to do 'research', which means go down to the tatty old library and use the ancient computers to look up stuff we don't even care about.

Reader 2: I wish I could go to school all day instead of just for an hour a day. School is just so amazing. You get to hear about all the incredible things in the world, and how things work, and what happened in the past and how people live all around the world and all that kind of thing. I can put everything I learn to good use right now. We don't have many books in our school, and the ones we have are a bit old and frayed – but the stuff in them is just so interesting. Our teacher tells us what he knows, but we have sixty pupils in the class and only about twenty books, so it's a bit difficult sometimes…

Reader 1: Got detention today. First off, I didn't have a pencil – the teacher's got hundreds in the cupboard – then I decided that last night I wanted to watch the football instead of doing some pointless bit of homework about some war that happened hundreds of years ago. They could all save themselves a lot of trouble if they just gave us pencils and didn't get so worked up about asking us to waste our time doing more work at home.

Reader 2: Whenever I can, I try to remember the things I learn at school when I am at home. I ask my Mum and Dad questions about the things we've been doing at school all the time. But they didn't go to school at all and so they can't help me very much. I heard about a far-away country today. It's called Scotland. Their schools sound like Heaven…

Talking and listening

- Do you find school boring or pointless?
- Do you think you appreciate school enough (or at all)?
- Are you lucky to have the education you are receiving?
- What do you think school is for?
- If school wasn't compulsory, would you attend?

The right to an education

The UN Declaration on the Rights of the Child says that everyone should have the right to a free education to help them become all that they can be. Right now you are probably sitting in a school where there are plenty of books, computers, DVD players and all sorts of technology. There are probably science labs and sports facilities and places to create art and cook food. You probably have teachers who are well qualified and dedicated to their jobs. Your school will be safe and clean, and all sorts of people – members of the Scottish Government, school inspectors, teachers, parents, cleaners and janitors – will play their part in making school the best it can be. Your education is probably free and, even if it's not, you could have a free education if you wanted to. You're probably given all the materials you need, from jotters to art materials and sports equipment. The UN says that this is your right. Are you grateful for it? Do you show that gratitude?

Active Learning

1. Draw up a 'Thank You' charter. You could make it look like a very official document with a seal etc. On this, write all the things that you're grateful about in your school. These should be displayed for all to see.

2. Work out how much your education actually costs. You might need to research this a little, but you should include things like how much all the staff of your school are paid in total, how much the upkeep of the building is per year, how much is spent on books and pencils etc. Now divide that by the number of pupils in your school and come up with a figure. You might be surprised how expensive your education is. You should display your calculations – perhaps in the form of graphs and charts. If that's all too much, choose one object like pencils and try to work out how much money is spent by your school on them each year.

3. Find out about a school in a country where education is either not free or very difficult to get access to. Perhaps as a school you could raise money to help out. On the Internet you will find examples of organisations trying to help educate children who don't have access to education (sometimes by building schools in the first place!). You could try an organisation such as Save the Children (www. savethechildren.org.uk).

→

4. For a day, get your school to act as if you were living in a country where education was much less well provided than it is in Scotland. Write about what it was like – your local newspaper might be interested in this!

5. How much choice do you have about what you learn in school? How much choice should you have? Think about arguments for and against greater choice for pupils about what they learn.

 Progress Check

1. Discuss these statements in class:
   a. 'No child should be forced to go to school.'
   b. 'In school you should get to choose your subjects right from first year (or Primary 1).'
   c. 'You should have to buy your own books and jotters for school.'
   d. 'Pupils who don't want to learn should be banned from going to school.'

2. Imagine the Scottish Government decided to charge everyone for sending their children to school. In what ways would this change Scottish society? Would it be fair?

3. In Scotland, state schools are paid for through people paying tax. Should people who do not have children have to pay for other people's children to go to school? Have a debate about this in class.

4. Two stars and a wish! Think about your own school and give it two stars for two things that are good about it and make a wish for something you'd like to see changed.

On your own

1. Free the Children believe in helping children through education. Visit its website (www.freethechildren.com) and write a short report about what it does. Another organisation that does similar work is Build a School (www.buildaschool.co.uk).

2. Other organisations think that the education of children is very important. Sometimes these organisations are based on religious belief. Search the following sites and see if any mention is made of the right to an education: Christianity (www.christianaid.org.uk), Islam (www.muslimaid.org), Humanism (www.humanism-scotland.org.uk).

3. Imagine you were given enough money to build a school for children in the developing world. Design the building and explain what would be taught there.

Sam has just moved from Edinburgh to Glasgow. He's finding things a bit different: he can't get used to being asked if he wants salt and vinegar on his fish supper, and he can't understand why his new schoolmates all ask for a 'piece' in the school canteen (a piece of what?). Sitting in class, he's about to get into a discussion with Ally and Billy – born and bred Glaswegians – that he's really not prepared for…

Ally: Hulawrerr, wee Sammy boy, howzitgaun? Ur ye cumin tae watch ra march the morra?

Sam: Sorry, what did you say?

Billy: C'moan Ally – he's no goat aw ra Glesga lingo yit huzee?

Ally: Naw, rightenuff. So, wee Sammy boy, ah'll dae it wan merr time, bit ah'll talk like they dae in Embrugh – aw posh n'at – now young Samuel, are you coming to watch the parade tomorrow afternoon?

Sam: What parade? Is it like the Festival parade with floats and fire jugglers and bands? I loved that when it came along Princes Street.

Ally: Well no, it's not quite like that young Samuel. There will undoubtedly be a band however, and drummers and small children dressed in bow ties…

Billy: And men with bowler hats and umbrellas.

Sam: Is it going to rain?

Ally: I am uncertain about that young Samuel. No, no, you seem to misapprehend – this is a parade of the Grand Orange Order of Scotland. A celebration of our identity and a defence of the freedoms gained for us by good King William of Orange.

Sam: But William's not the King yet.

Billy: No, young Samuel, you remain misguided. We are conversing about King William the third of the House of Orange and his defence of the Protestant faith in 1690 and so forth. Anyway, the march tomorrow is a celebration of our Protestant heritage…

Ally: The upholding of the constitution of our nation…

Billy: The protection of our freedom.

Sam: And all of this just by doing a march? Glasgow's quite some place.

Ally: Yes, indeed it is young man from the east…

A protest for religious groups to come together in Glasgow

Freedom of speech

Free speech means expressing your point of view openly in words and actions, provided that doing so doesn't harm anyone. There are many Orange parades in Scotland every year. These happen almost entirely in the central belt and the majority take place in the west. Like Ally and Billy, supporters of these events say that they are a celebration and defence of their way of life. People who are against them say that they are based on beliefs that are bigoted – meaning that they discriminate against other people, in particular Roman Catholic people. They say that such marches should be banned because they stir up anger between Catholics and Protestants in the community. But supporters of the marches deny that they're trying to offend people. In modern Scotland, the law says that you can't just say anything about anyone. Freedom of speech is important, but sometimes we can't do whatever we want. Should events such as Orange marches be banned?

🗨 Talking and listening

- Have you ever seen an Orange march (or been in one)? What are they like?
- Some people say that marches like Orange parades should be banned. Do you think anyone's beliefs should be banned?
- Should you always respect someone's beliefs – even if you strongly disagree with them?
- Free speech means being able to say anything you like, but in Scotland there are laws about what you can and cannot say. What things do you think these laws cover?
- Should you be able to say (or do) anything you like if it is your belief?

⚙ Active Learning

1. Find out about the arguments for and against the Orange marches. Copy and complete the following table, adding as many rows as you can.

Arguments for Orange marches	Arguments against Orange marches
The marches are nothing more than a celebration of identity	The marches are a way of publicly criticising another group – namely Catholics
The marches are friendly family events with music and colour	The marches lead to trouble by stirring up disagreements in Scottish society

➡

2. In some countries, governments do not allow free speech. People are often sent to jail because they speak out against their governments. These people are called political prisoners. Organisations like Amnesty International (**www.amnesty.org.uk**) work to help them. Find out about Amnesty, what it believes and what it does. You could create an information leaflet or a display of your findings.

3. The opposite of freedom of speech is censorship, whereby things are banned or controlled. Here are some examples of censorship as they happen in Scotland today. Discuss each one and express your views on it. Is this kind of censorship right?
   a. bleeping out swear words on TV programmes at certain times
   b. not advertising certain products on TV (like cigarettes)
   c. schools not allowing you access to certain websites
   d. certificates on films and computer games
   e. 'parental advisory' notices on music.

4. What things are censored or limited in your area? Why does that happen? Is it right? Find examples and explore the arguments that people have about this. What views do you have?

5. There's an episode of *The Simpsons* where Bart encourages everyone to do exactly what they want. It ends up in chaos. What rules does a society need to work properly?

On your own

1. Parents can buy computer programs that monitor what their children look at on the Internet. Is this right? Find some adults who agree with this and others who don't. What arguments do they use? (It might be best not to ask your own parents if they do this – you might not like their answer!)

2. What is the TV watershed? Find out about the rules linked to it. What do you think about it?

3. Do you think children have enough freedom to express their point of view in Scotland today? Do a survey of people your age and present your findings in a short report with graphs and charts.

Progress Check

1. Here are three statements. Discuss them in class and decide which one you agree with most. (It could be that you agree with more than one.)
   a. 'People should be free to say and do whatever they want.'
   b. 'People should sometimes be free to say and do what they want, but sometimes banned from doing so.'
   c. 'What people say and do should be strictly controlled by the government.'

2. In the book *1984* by George Orwell, the main character lives in a society where CCTV cameras follow your every move. 'Big Brother' is watching and there is no real free speech. How would your life change if Big Brother started watching everything you did? Could things like Google Streetmap and CCTV cameras in public places mean that Big Brother is already watching us? Discuss this in class.

3. Imagine you became the First Minister of Scotland. What things would you ban? What would you 'un-ban'?

4. Censorship is different around the world. Find one example of something that is allowed in Scotland but might not be allowed in another country.

Katie has a pony, its name is thunder bay
It cost more than two thousand pounds so she rides it every day
Shona walks to school cos her mum's not got a car
Its just as well the journey isn't really all that far
Katie has a bungalow surrounded by nice ground
And a very pricey clarinet, which makes a decent sound
Shona's in a high-rise flat with not much of a view
And nothing much to call her own and nothing much to do
Katie goes on holiday to Paris and to Rome
Shona's never been abroad and rarely leaves her home
Katie dines with family at a table spread so fine
And sometimes mummy lets her have a sip of top-class wine
Shona sorts her own tea out, most often microwaved
Or leftovers from last night in their carton or tin saved
Katie has a wardrobe full of dresses, tops and shoes
And party gowns so princess-like from which she has to choose
Shona has a few clothes which she wears until they're through
Which mostly were his sister's, who liked grotty shades of blue
Katie's room is filled with stuff, the best that can be bought
Computers, cameras, toys and games – in fact she's got the lot
Shona's room is stark and bare with just a few small things
Hair brushes bought at jumble sales and tacky fake gold rings
Katie has a tutor to help her with her learning
Shona struggles on her own so that one day she'll be earning
To help her mum out with the bills and keep the kids well fed
For mum works all the hours there are, then collapses into bed
Katie knows that she will always have her happiness and wealth
A great big car, a lovely home, good food, nice things, good health
Shona's not so sure about the future life she'll lead
The same tired flat, the miserable life – and kids of her own to feed?
There's little chance that these two girls are ever going to meet
Even though their lives are lived so close
At either end
Of one street

Talking and listening

- What evidence is there in your area of people who have lots of money and people who don't?
- Does having money make people happy?
- In what ways is life different for people who have money and people who are poor?
- Why are some people poor and some people rich?
- Should rich people help the poor?

Rich and poor in Scotland

It's sometimes easy to think that poverty only exists in far-off countries. Even in our own communities we can see evidence of people who have a lot more than others. How does this happen? Do poor people not work as hard as rich people, or have they just not been as lucky? Poverty is a very complicated matter, with much more than one simple cause. Maybe not doing well at school leads to a poorly paid job, or maybe you lose your job.

When you are poor you are more likely to have poor health and a more difficult life. You might feel hopeless about the future and unhappy. The UN Declaration of Human Rights says that everyone should have the right to economic security. This means that no matter who you are or where you live, you have the right not to live in poverty. Governments should do all they can to end poverty. But can they do everything? What about individuals? What should we do to end poverty in Scotland and the world?

Active Learning

1. Find out what kinds of poverty there are and what the effects are. Split your class into two groups. One group should look at poverty in Scotland and the other should look at poverty in another country – perhaps in the developing world. Your project should include:
   a. facts and figures about poverty in your chosen country
   b. images of poverty
   c. your own writing about the causes and effects of poverty
   d. your own views about how poverty might be ended.
   You could use the following section headings:
   a. what is poverty?
   b. some possible causes of poverty
   c. the effects of poverty
   d. what can be done to help the poor.

2. As a class, raise some money for a charity that helps the poor. Lots of fund-raising ideas can be found on charity websites. Perhaps the whole school could get involved?

3. Find out about the north–south divide. On a world map, draw the north–south dividing line and explain what this is all about. You could include text, images and statistics.

4. Many religious, as well as non-religious people, believe that fighting against poverty is very important. Choose one religion and one non-religious group, and explore their views about poverty and how to fight it. Create a display board with one side each for each view. You could organise your information like this:
   a. What does this group believe the causes of poverty are?
   b. Why does this group think we should help the poor?
   c. What does this group do to help the poor?

5. Some people believe that you can be happy without having material possessions. Is this true?

![Progress Check icon] **Progress Check**

1. Some people think that we should help the poor at home before we help those in other countries. What do you think? Write the words 'Charity begins at home' on a wall and let people add their own responses.

2. Imagine that one day Katie and Shona do meet. What might they ask each other about their lives? What might they learn? Write the script of a conversation the two girls might have.

3. Write up your own action plan. 'Three things I could do to help the poor… today'.

4. Here are some reasons why some people think we should help the poor. Which of them do you think is the 'best' reason? Why do you think so?
   a. Helping the poor is just right.
   b. Helping the poor makes the world a safer place.
   c. Helping the poor makes me feel good about myself.
   d. Helping the poor makes me feel less guilty about how wealthy I am.
   e. Helping the poor makes me look good.

![On your own icon] **On your own**

1. Are there any societies or groups where there is no such thing as rich and poor? Find out.

2. What do people you know do to help the poor? Carry out some confidential interviews and report on your findings.

3. Think about the skills and abilities you have. How could you use them to help the poor?

Fact: Women are still, on average, paid much less than men – even when they are doing the same job.

Fact: Women are still much less likely to reach the top jobs in Scotland than men are.

Fact: Women around the world who work full-time are still far more likely to do most of the housework too.

Fact: In many countries, girls receive little education compared to boys.

Fact: In some countries, women are treated by the law as if they are the 'property' of their husbands.

Fact: In some countries, women are punished severely for doing certain things. Men in the same countries receive far lighter punishment for doing the same things.

Fact: In some countries, women are forced to wear certain types of clothing and punished harshly if they do not.

Fact: Women are far more likely to suffer physical abuse in a relationship than men are.

Fact: Women are still used in advertising to sell things in ways that men are not.

Fact: Many men still think that a woman's place is in the home.

Fact: In some situations and places in Scotland, women are banned from doing certain things that men are allowed to do.

Fact: In some countries, girls are killed shortly after birth because their parents see girls as a 'burden' to a family, not a 'benefit' like a boy.

Fact: Some jobs are still seen as 'men's work'.

Fact: In some countries, girls are more likely to be sold into slavery than boys.

Fact: All of these things are still happening in the world… right now.

Talking and listening

In groups of boys only and girls only

- Should men and women be treated as equals?
- What evidence is there that they are not treated equally?
- Does anyone in your group think that men and women should be treated differently?
- Has anyone in your group been treated unfairly because they are a boy or a girl?

Then in mixed groups of boys and girls

- Discuss the questions above again and listen carefully to each other's views. Make sure that you express your view reasonably.

The rights of women

It's sad but true that in the twenty-first century women are still sometimes treated in very negative ways. They do not always have equality at home or at work, and they still suffer things that men don't. This can start from childhood, with boys getting better opportunities than girls, and can continue right into adulthood. Why are women still treated differently to men, in Scotland and overseas? In Scotland, there are laws against treating women differently to men but sometimes these laws are not followed. Other times the laws don't apply. For example, in some towns in the Borders, it is often preferred that women do not take part in the Common Riding. Some clubs and groups do not allow women to join. Women still suffer in many different ways at the hands of men, and sometimes the law does not protect them very well. The UN Declaration on Human Rights says that no one should be treated unfairly because they are male or female, and yet it still happens. Why do women still suffer from discrimination and bad treatment?

Active Learning

1. Choose one of the Fact statements on page 46 and create your own piece of artwork that illustrates this idea.

2. Choose a different Fact and carry out your own research into it, perhaps using the Internet. Produce an in-depth article on this for a teenage magazine. Make sure your readers know:
   a. what the issue is
   b. where in the world this happens
   c. what beliefs and attitudes are behind it
   d. how governments, groups or organisations are trying to change it
   e. what the reader could do to help change it.

3. Some people say that women get a bad deal because of how religions treat them. However, followers of these religions reply that they are not treating women badly, just differently. Here are some issues about the rights of women that you can find in Scotland:
   a. women in Islam wearing the traditional veil (burka)
   b. women in Roman Catholic Christianity who are not allowed to be priests
   c. women in Hinduism or Islam who may have their marriages arranged
   d. women in some Scottish Christian groups who are only allowed to have certain roles in their church or must dress in certain ways

→

e. women in the Orthodox Jewish faith who must sit apart from the men and cannot do certain things in the synagogue.

In groups, choose one of these issues, and then:

a. Find out what the main issue is.

b. Investigate the arguments for and against treating women in this way.

c. Express your own views on the issue.

If possible, invite people from the relevant faith communities to come and talk to the class. Ideally you could talk to two people from the same faith who disagree about the role of women in their religion.

4. Some men think that they are starting to be treated unfairly. What issues might they be talking about? Try searching for 'men's rights' on the Internet. In what ways are the issues the same as for women, and in what ways do they differ?

5. Discuss this issue with your history teacher. How have women's rights improved over the last 100 years or so? How did these changes come about?

 **Progress Check**

1. Have a class debate: 'A woman's place is wherever she wants it to be'.

2. Choose one statement or view expressed in this section. Now express your own point of view about it. Make sure that you explain the reasons for your views as clearly as possible.

3. Design a poster about one of the issues you have looked at in this section. The poster should express the view that women should not be discriminated against.

4. 'If I could…' Write down some things you could do in your life to improve the treatment of women in the world. Who knows, perhaps you are a future First Minister or world leader who'll be able to put them into action one day…

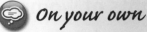 *On your own*

1. Carry out some interviews with your family about the rights of women. Are any of the views explored in this section held at home? Be sensitive to people's views, and if you report your findings do so without naming names. Try to let people give you their views without judging them too much. You don't need to agree with what they say, but it is important to listen and to try to understand it.

2. Find one news article about the treatment of women either in Scotland or abroad. Put this into your jotter and explain what you think about it.

3. Find out about one organisation that works for equality for women. What does it do and why does it do it?

Winter celebrations

4

This week's edition of the TV game show Universally Challenged sees Potter's College Oxford face the University of Clydebank. The new presenter, Desmond Danderhall, is about to ask the first question…

Desmond: So, for your starter for ten. What is the name given by Scots to New Year celebrations? [*Buzz*]

Announcer: Potter's, Hendley-Atkinson:

Potter's student 1: Burns day?

Desmond: No. Anyone from Clydebank? [*Buzz*]

Clydebank student 1: Hogmanay.

Desmond: Correct. Another starter for ten. What is the name given to the first person to arrive at the door at Hogmanay? [*Buzz*]

Announcer: Potter's, Wilkinson:

Potter's student 2: Jimmy?

Desmond: [*With a twisted face*] For goodness sake… anyone from Clydebank?

Clydebank student 2: The first foot.

Desmond: Well done Clydebank, I can now offer you three more questions on Hogmanay celebrations. First, what object might be placed on a white tablecloth at Hogmanay?

Clydebank student 1: A Rikki Fulton book?

Desmond: Well, it seems that the Scottish team are clueless about their own customs. No, it's a piece of coal. Next question: what's the name of the cake that is traditionally served up at Hogmanay?

Clydebank student 3: Dundee cake?

Desmond: Dundee cake?! I thought you were supposed to be highly educated people? No, it's black bun. Your final question: what song is traditionally sung at Hogmanay?

Clydebank student 2: [*Confidently*] 'Ye cannae shove your granny aff a bus'.

Desmond: No, it's 'Auld lang syne'. Right, I'm going to ask another starter question, although I'm beginning to wonder why I bother. What traditional toast is made at Hogmanay? [*Buzz*]

Announcer: Potter's, Hendley-Atkinson:

Potter's student 1: Thick toast with butter?

Desmond: Oh I give up. No, it's 'Lang may yer lum reek'. Last question, then I'm going home. What have the bells got to do with Hogmanay? [*Buzz*]

Announcer: Clydebank, McGarrity-O'Donnelly:

Clydebank student 2: It's a kind of whisky.

Desmond: Right, I've had enough. I thought you were supposed to be the smartest young people in the country? If you ever start running the place, then we're in trouble! Thank you and good night.

Hogmanay

For lots of people, the only thing they do at Hogmanay is watch TV until just after midnight and then go to bed. But in Edinburgh there's usually a giant street party in Princes Street and at midnight there's a big fireworks display with pipe bands on the floodlit ramparts of Edinburgh Castle. This comes at the end of a week of celebrations involving a torch-lit parade and sometimes a big bonfire on Calton Hill. Around Scotland, people wish each other a 'Guid New Year'. They think about the year that has just passed and make their New Year resolutions. It's a time when people try to make a new start in their lives. Of course, for some it is just a party with a lot of drinking and over-eating. Do you think it's important to have a point in the year where we all try to 'start again'?

Active Learning

1. How do you and your family celebrate Hogmanay? Do you do keep any of the old traditions? Write about what happens.

2. Do you make New Year resolutions? Did you make any last year? Did you keep them? Carry out a survey in your class to find out what different New Year resolutions people made and how well they stuck to them.

3. Find out about the traditions linked to Hogmanay that were mentioned in the *Universally Challenged* show. Create a display of your findings. You could look at:
   a. cleaning the ashes from the fire (sometimes cleaning your whole house)
   b. settling your debts
   c. the first foot being tall and dark (and handsome!)
   d. the lump of coal on the table (sometimes a loaf of bread too).

4. Fire is an important part of Hogmanay celebrations around Scotland. In the Western Isles there's an old tradition of the smoking stick being carried around to ward off evil. In Stonehaven, people walk through the town swinging huge balls of fire in preparation for Hogmanay (see www.stonehavenfireballs.co.uk). Do your own display or project about the use of fire at Hogmanay. You could either focus on one celebration or look at how fire is used across a few different ones. Why do you think there are a lot of activities involving fire at this time of year?

5. Hogmanay is about reflecting on the year just past and planning for the year ahead. What has been good about the year so far? What would you like to do better next year?

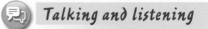

Talking and listening

- Does your family and/ or community keep any Hogmanay traditions?
- Why do people celebrate at Hogmanay?
- What do you like and dislike about Hogmanay?
- Should people keep traditions – even if they don't understand why they are doing them?

1. Here are three statements. For each one, discuss in class and write your own views about it.
   a. 'It is important to keep traditions because they help us understand who we are.'
   b. 'We should only keep traditions when we know what the traditions mean, otherwise there's no point.'
   c. 'Keeping traditions is just for older people.'

4. If you have ever attended a fire procession or something similar, write a story about what happened. Try to describe what you saw in all its detail as well as how it made you feel. If you haven't been to one, have a look on YouTube (**www.youtube.com/watch?v=xgUOX1qVpsw**).

5. What do all the Hogmanay fire festival events have in common? What does this tell us about how people feel at this time of year?

On your own

1. Find out about the Up Helly Aa event in Shetland. This doesn't happen at Hogmanay but has a lot of features in common with the New Year fire celebrations. See **www.uphellyaa.org** for information or watch video footage at **www.youtube.com/watch?v=nWcXzcssJAY**. You could print a picture from the event and write an explanation of what happens and why.

2. Have a look at the history of Hogmanay celebrations on the Internet. What has changed? What has stayed the same? What things do you think will still be going in 100 years?

3. When Scottish people move abroad they still seem to want to keep some of the old traditions going. What do they do and why do they do this? Prepare a short information sheet about the Scottish community in Nova Scotia, Canada (see **www.chebucto.ns.ca/Heritage/FSCNS/ScotsHome.html**) or the Scottish community in New Zealand (see **www.electricscotland.com/history/nz**).

A group of first years are sitting in a Maths class at a Scottish secondary school. They are working out some basic differential calculus, but all they can think about is Christmas…

Reader 1: What you all getting for Christmas?

Reader 4: I'm getting a new Xbox and loads of games.

Reader 3: A laptop, a plasma-screen TV and an iPod touch.

Reader 1: I'm getting my presents in the Caribbean this year. We're going to be lying on a tropical beach on Christmas day, sunning ourselves and dipping into the clear blue ocean.

Reader 2: Not very Christmassy, is it?

Reader 1: Who cares? I'll still get my stuff.

Reader 3: Yeah, I suppose. Anyone remember what they got for Christmas last year?

[Everybody hums and haws and mumbles, but nobody can actually remember]

Reader 4: Can't wait until the holiday.

Reader 3: Yeah, but it's only two weeks – and we only stop two days before Christmas

Reader 4: My parents always let me skive off a few days

before, though. There's too much to do to get ready for it all.

Reader 2: Tell me about it. You'd think my Mum was going to crack up about Christmas. Got to get the right turkey, the right potatoes, and engage in combat in Asda to get Brussels sprouts. *[Everyone disgusted, yuck etc.]*

Reader 1: Yeah, my parents are always fighting in the kitchen about how long the turkey's got to go, or the rest of the happy family are arguing about politics or religion or whatever – in their paper hats and filled with too much drink.

Reader 3: The whole thing's just a pain really. Nobody seems to enjoy it – everybody gets stressed out and nobody believes in it anyway. Maybe we should just ban it. *[Everyone shocked and protests against this idea]*

Reader 1: But then we wouldn't get our stuff. *[Everyone expresses agreement]*

Reader 4: Never mind, only three months to go…

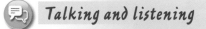
Talking and listening

- When do your preparations for Christmas begin?
- Do you think Christmas is too stressful?
- Why does your family celebrate Christmas?
- Do you think there's any point in celebrating Christmas?
- How much do you know about why Christmas is celebrated?

Christmas

Christmas is celebrated for many different reasons. The Christian faith celebrates 25 December as the day when Jesus came to Earth. For them, it is a celebration of the Incarnation – which means that God became a human and lived a human life to save us from our sinful ways. The idea was to show humans how to live and so put right the failed relationship between God and his creation. Christmas marks the start of the whole Christian faith, and many of the stories about Jesus's birth are believed to teach us important things about who he was and why he came to Earth. Many of the things we do at Christmas are linked to symbols in the Christian story – like giving each other presents to remind us that God gave us the gift of his only son. Of course, many people who are not Christians celebrate Christmas too. They enjoy the holiday, the presents and the good food. They like the chance to see family and cheer themselves up in the dark winter months. Does it matter why we celebrate Christmas?

Active Learning

1. Find out about the Christmas story and tell it in your own way. You can do this as a drama, a puppet show, a PowerPoint presentation – or you could make a video or a story board. You could also illustrate the Christmas story from the Bible with a series of pictures.

2. Find out why the Christian faith decided to use 25 December to celebrate the birth of Jesus. Write about what you find. (Clue: look up 'Saturnalia' on the Internet.)

3. Take a selection of Christmas cards (or do a survey in your local shops if it's the right time of year). Sort them into two groups: those that are linked to the Christmas story and those that are not. How many are in each category? Produce some charts and graphs to display your findings. Which cards do people in your class like best and why do they like these? Which cards are unpopular? You could design the ideal Christmas card.

4. How do people celebrate Christmas around Scotland and around the world? Design a poster – 'Christmas around Scotland' or 'Christmas around the World'. Describe some of the customs and how the event is celebrated. There may be people in your own school who have links with other parts of Scotland or other countries – ask them about their experiences. At the end, you could have a Christmas celebration in your class that reflects the customs and traditions of another country.

5. Many people believe that Christmas is an especially important time to help those in need. What things are done at Christmas to help others? Find out what the Salvation Army (**www.salvationarmy.org. uk**) does at Christmas.

1. Have a class discussion about this statement, or sit in a circle and express a view about it without others commenting. 'You should only celebrate Christmas if you are a Christian.'

2. Choose a selection of Christmas symbols from the Christmas cards. Explain what each symbol is and how it might help people in their understanding of or celebration of Christmas.

3. Describe, in your own words, two different Christmas customs around the world.

On your own

1. Santa Claus is a popular figure at Christmas. He started as a Christian bishop in Asia and is now a jolly fat man in a red and white suit. How did this change come about? Write a short illustrated report about what you find.

2. Interview some friends and family about Christmas. What do they like about it and what do they not like? Why do they celebrate it? How important is religious belief?

3. Some people argue that Christmas is becoming too commercialised. This means that it is just about selling stuff. Do a survey of your local shops and find out when they started to put up their Christmas displays. Perhaps you could also ask the shop owners/managers why they put their Christmas displays out when they do.

18 Hanukkah

Benjamin, 12, Jerusalem: 28th day of Kislev, around 165 BCE (BC)

Antiochus was a great King of Syria – or so he thought. But if you ask me he was just a big bully – trying to force people to do things his way because he was bigger and more powerful than them. He tried to force us to ignore G-d and worship silly statues from Greece. When we Jews refused to bow down to his statues he did something even more idiotic. He had a statue of himself made and expected us to bow down to that, as if he was a god himself. Talk about full of yourself! Some brave Jews called the Maccabees decided that they'd had enough of this and rebelled. They tried to stop Antiochus turning our holiest Temple in our great capital Jerusalem into a disgusting place full of offensive statues. We Jews do not worship statues – we never have. The Maccabees were willing to risk their lives to protect our beliefs and our way of life, and they fought

hard against Antiochus and his armies. Eventually they won, but in the battles our Temple was destroyed. Once we had rebuilt the Temple and dedicated it back to G-d, a great big candlestick was lit – well it was actually eight candlesticks all joined into one. It didn't use candles though; it was kept burning using holy oil. There wasn't much oil left in the Temple, except for one wee tiny pot. But that wee tiny pot kept the flames on the candlestick alight for eight whole days. We believe that this was a little miracle sent by G-d to remind us that he had protected us. I wonder if people will remember these events in years to come?

Rebecca, 12, Dundee: 12th December 2009 CE (AD)

Today is the Festival of Hanukkah. Jews all over the world remember the defeat of Antiochus by the Maccabees long ago. We remember how the menorah stayed alight by a miracle of G-d and

this in turn reminds us that just as G-d looked after us then he looks after us now. We light a Hanukkah – one light a day for eight days to remember the events long ago. But we also give gifts – especially to children. We eat lots of things cooked in oil – not very healthy, I know – to remind us how the holy oil lasted so long (longer than the tasty latkes Mum makes, anyway!). We play games using a dreidel, which is a wee spinning top. Its letters stand for 'a miracle happened here'. We also eat special doughnuts called sufganiyot – I love them! The whole event reminds us that even in the darkest times in Jewish history, G-d was there with us – as he'll always be.

Hanukkah

Jewish people believe it is important to remember how events in the past help us in the present. The history of the Jewish people has not been an easy one, and yet their faith survives to this day. Hanukkah is a reminder to Jewish people that G-d has chosen them and that he will not ignore them when they are in need. Hanukkah takes place at slightly different times each year, but it's always during the dark winter months. It uses the lights of the Hanukkah menorah as symbols that G-d lights up even the darkest times in our lives. When things seem dark and dismal to you, what lights up your life?

Active Learning

1. You'll see that throughout this section the word God has been written as G-d. This is to respect Jewish beliefs. Find out why Jewish people write G-d when writing in English. What is the Hebrew name for G-d? When a Jewish person reads this Hebrew name, what will he or she say instead? Why? Design an information sheet about this. The Hebrew word for G-d is on page 56.

2. Make your own Hanukkah menorah and light it over eight days. You could finish this off with a Hanukkah celebration in class, including playing with a dreidel, and eating latkes and sufganiyot. You can also find some Hanukkah songs at **www.chabad.org**.

3. Design and make your own Hanukkah cards and give them to friends and family. If you have any members of the Jewish faith in your school community they might especially welcome this recognition of their beliefs.

4. Hanukkah celebrates the victory of light over darkness. What things count as darkness in the world today? Design a collage of images from newspapers/magazines exploring darkness. You could draw a brightly lit Hanukkah menorah in the centre of your collage showing light overcoming darkness.

5. Write a letter to Benjamin. Tell him about how Hanukkah is celebrated in the twenty-first century. You could include some photos of your own school event if you had one.

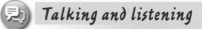

Talking and listening

- Hanukkah is a celebration of a miracle. What do you think a miracle is? Do you think they happen?
- Antiochus tried to stop the Jews from practising their religion and make them do things that were against their religion. Why do you think he did this?
- What things to bullies do to try to make people feel bad?
- Jewish people think it is important to remember events from their history. Why do you think that is? Do you think it is important to remember the past?
- In what ways is Hanukkah similar to Christmas and Hogmanay? In what ways is it different?

On your own

1. There are two other stories linked to Hanukkah. One is the story of the Priest Mattathias and the other is of Hannah and her sons. Find out about these stories.

2. Find out how the dreidel game is played and what its meaning is. You could make a little model dreidel and play the game according to its rules. Try looking at **www.chabad.org**.

3. Jewish people have had many periods of difficulty in their history. Find out a little about Jewish history and write a few sentences about it. The website **www.jewishhistory.org.il/history.php** provides a good timeline.

Progress Check

1. Here are some statements about Hanukkah. Discuss them in groups and decide which one you agree with and why.
   a. 'It is important to remember events that happened in the past.'
   b. 'We should forget about the past and live for the present.'
   c. 'Remembering the past helps you understand who you are.'
   d. 'A bully is a bully no matter where or when he lives.'
   e. 'It doesn't matter why you celebrate an event like Hanukkah – it's just a bit of fun.'

2. Although Jewish people believe that G-d looks after them, they also believe that humans have a responsibility to fight for what they believe in (just like the Maccabees did). What would people in your class be prepared to fight for? What would you fight for?

3. Some Jewish people in Scotland celebrate both Hanukkah and Christmas, and some celebrate only Hanukkah. Why is this? What would you do if you were a Jewish person? (If you are Jewish, what do you do and why?)

In the ancient city of Ayodhya, a great King sat and sobbed. One of his wives, Queen Kaikeyi, had made him promise to banish his favourite son Prince Rama to the forest for 14 years and to make her son, Prince Bharata, the heir to the throne. Rama obeyed his father's wishes and left the city for the forest along with his beautiful wife Sita and his brother Lakshman – who both volunteered to go so that Rama would not be alone.

The forest is a dangerous place, full of evil demons. One day Lakshman was off hunting and Rama heard him call for help. But Rama didn't want to leave Sita alone and so placed her inside a magic circle where she would be protected. Soon after Rama had gone, an old man came asking Sita for a cup of water. Sita felt so sorry for the old man that she stepped out of her protective circle to help him. Just then, he transformed into a many-headed evil demon known as Ravana. He whisked Sita off to his terrible fortress on the Island of Lanka. Meanwhile, Rama had discovered that Lakshman was fine – Ravana's evil demon sister had played a trick on them both. By the time he returned to where he had left, Sita was gone…

On Lanka, Ravana gave Sita a choice. She could either marry him or he would kill her, cook her

and eat her. He gave her a year to decide. During this time, Rama and Lakshman looked everywhere for Sita. One day they met Hanuman, the monkey king. He said he knew where Sita was and that he and his monkey army would help Rama rescue her. So they travelled to Lanka and there fought a mighty battle. At the end of the battle, Rama killed Ravana with a sacred bow and arrow.

Not only was Sita safe, but the 14 years of banishment were over and Rama could return to Ayodhya. But what would he find there? Would the people remember him after all this time? As they approached the city there was a trail of lights leading them towards the centre of the city. The people had remembered him and they welcomed him back as the rightful King. Kaikeyi's son had been ashamed by his mother's actions, and had placed Rama's slippers on the royal throne to await his return. Now he was here the throne could be returned to its rightful owner, Rama, King of Ayodhya.

Ever since that day people have celebrated the victory of Rama over the evil demon Ravana. They celebrate Rama's bravery and loyalty, his sense of duty. They celebrate the faithfulness of his wife Sita, and the courage and friendship of his brother Lakshman. They celebrate the idea that good will win over evil every time. Just as people set out lamps or diwas to welcome Rama's return, they still use lights to celebrate at this time of year – which is now known as Diwali, meaning 'row of lights'.

Diwali

Diwali celebrates this story, which is known as the Ramayana. It is a very popular story all over India. The festival is celebrated in October or November, as the nights begin to get darker. People light diwa lamps in their homes, just as the people of Ayodhya had lit the way home for Rama and Sita. This expresses the idea that the darkness of evil can be banished by the goodness of light. Hindus give each other gifts at this time of year and enjoy singing, dancing and eating special foods. In some parts of India, giant models of Ravana are set on fire. Also, at this time of year it is believed that the goddess Lakshmi will visit your house – but only if it is clean and you've got your diwa lamps out! She will bring you good luck for the year to come. As Diwali approaches people try to sort things out in their lives so they can start all over again afterwards. You might try to make up with someone you've fallen out with. If you're in business you'll sort out all your money affairs before Diwali arrives. It is a time for goodwill to all and new beginnings.

Active Learning

1. Retell the story of the Ramayana. You can do this in any format you like – from cartoon strip to drama, video-making or even a puppet show. Make sure that you don't just tell the story but try to explain the meaning behind it too.

2. Rama, Sita, Lakshman and Hanuman are thought of as heroes in Hinduism. Who are modern-day heroes? Connect the heroism of the characters in the Ramayana with modern heroes and make a display of your work. You could use the following ideas: bravery/courage; loyalty; duty; faithfulness; friendship; determination…

3. The characters in the Ramayana symbolise light fighting against darkness. Which groups or individuals are the lights fighting against the darkness in today's world? Create a collage and explain why you have chosen these particular people or groups.

4. Imagine a film was being made of the Ramayana (there are many!). Who would you choose to play the parts? Explain the reasons for your choices.

Talking and listening

- Does good always defeat evil?
- Are you a brave and loyal person? Do you know people who are?
- Which character in this story do you like best? Why?
- Do you think Rama should have persuaded his father to ignore Kaikeyi's demands?
- Why do you think Lakshman and Sita went with Rama? Would you have gone?

Progress Check

1. The Ramayana is believed by many Hindus to be a factually true story. Some believe that it is a myth – a story with a meaning. Do you think it matters whether the story actually happened or not? Discuss in groups and report your views.

2. In what ways are the celebrations of Christmas, Hanukkah and Diwali similar? How are they different?

3. Find out how Hindus prepare their homes for Diwali. Describe how you would prepare your home.

On your own

1. In Unit 1 (Beliefs), *Star Wars* and the Jedi Knights were mentioned. There are some interesting similarities between the first *Star Wars* movie and the Ramayana. See how well you can match up the characters and story. (You can find the *Star Wars* plotline at **www.imdb. com/title/tt0076759/ plotsummary**.)

2. The Ramayana is not only a very popular story – it is also a very popular comic book that children love to read. If you're near any shops, try to get hold of one and bring it into class to discuss – if not, you can find examples of pages on the Internet.

3. At Diwali, children often design colourful rangoli patterns to welcome Lakshmi. Find examples of rangoli patterns and design your own or copy one that you find.

20 Samhain

It's Alva in the foothills of the Campsie Fells, where they sometimes say that the hills have eyes… it's also 31 October and two first years are discussing the night ahead…

Kelly: You going guising tonight?

Anya: No, I'll be busy tonight.

Kelly: Busy? What… you got a party you're not telling me about?

Anya: No, it's Samhain and my family will be celebrating it in the usual way.

Kelly: So what do you do?

Anya: Well it's two things really – it's the Celtic New Year.

Kelly: I didn't know you were a Celtic supporter?

Anya: I'm not, it's the New Year celebrations of the Celtic people of this country. The ancient Celts… you know. *[Kelly looks blankly at Anya – she obviously doesn't know]* Anyway, we believe that this night marks the end of the summer season and the beginning of the dark winter months. It's us kind of getting ready for winter. We also remember the dead.

Kelly: Whoa! Are you going all Goth on me now?

Anya: We believe that on this night the curtain between the world of the living and the dead is at its thinnest, and the spirits of the dead can come and join the spirits of the living.

Kelly: You're freaking me out a bit here girl.

Anya: No need for that. We don't get miserable about the dead – or fear them. We think that death is just another thing that happens to you. In fact, we invite the dead to join our celebrations.

Kelly: So do you dance around bonfires and stuff too?

Anya: Way too cold round here for that kind of stuff, but sometimes we light bonfires to warm us up and remind us of the warmth of summer. In the past, people would have a big feast too – maybe roast an animal or two on the fire to fill their bellies before the cold winter comes.

Kelly: Now it sounds like Christmas.

Anya: Yeah, I see what you mean…

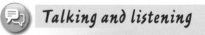 **Talking and listening**

- What do you do at Hallowe'en? Why?
- Do you think the dead are 'still around' in any way?
- How easy is it to remember the summer months when the winter has arrived?
- Who were the Celts? How much do you know about them?
- Are any of the features of Samhain celebrated where you live?

Samhain

Anya has told you a lot about Samhain. It is an old Celtic festival that is probably the origin of lots of our modern-day Hallowe'en customs. The dead were remembered and celebrated and it was believed that the living and dead could mingle on this day. It was also believed that the dead could help people to tell the future, and an ancient group called Druids did lots of fortune-telling at this time of year. This was also a time when people prepared themselves for the coming winter months. There wasn't much grazing left so many animals were killed, providing meat to last through the winter. Their bones were burned in great heaps – some think that this is the origin of the word bon(e)fire. At this time of year people turned towards the dark months and got ready to try to survive them. In modern Scotland, pagans still celebrate Samhain in traditional ways.

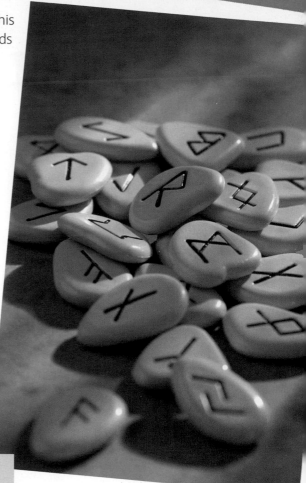

Paganism is a set of beliefs that follow three principles:

- honour nature and all life
- harm no one
- recognise the divine in everything (see **www. scottishpf.org/princ.html**).

Pagans believe in trying to live in harmony with nature as much as possible. Samhain is a celebration of the natural world and its importance. How important do you think nature is?

Active Learning

1. Find out more about Samhain. What is done and why? You could compare this with modern Hallowe'en celebrations. Design a project or a PowerPoint display about what you find.

2. Paganism is all about reverence for nature. Prepare a factsheet on this belief system. You could look at the website of the Scottish Pagan Federation (**www.scottishpf.org**) for ideas. On this site there are links to all sorts of other Pagan groups; there is also general information about Paganism on the BBC website (**www.bbc.co.uk/religion/religions/paganism**).

3. Samhain was a time for predicting the future. Try out some of the traditional techniques if you like. One was peeling an apple while thinking about the person you would marry. You have to try to get the peel off in one go. Then you throw the peel over your shoulder. The peel is supposed to land in the shape of a letter of the alphabet. This letter tells you who you will marry! See if you can find other ways of predicting the future and try them out.

4. Some people in Scotland are very opposed to the celebration of Hallowe'en. Find out why this is. What are their arguments and what do you think about them? You could interview people about this if possible (and try to present both sides of the argument).

1. Some believe that at Samhain (and Hallowe'en) the dead and the living are better able to communicate. What do you think of this idea? Discuss it in class and think of two arguments that would support this belief and two arguments that might oppose it.

2. Some of the customs that we celebrate at Hallowe'en were originally Samhain customs. Choose two or three Hallowe'en customs and link them up with the Samhain traditions that came before them. You could also look at some Hallowe'en customs that originated in the USA, such as Jack O'Lanterns.

3. Imagine you were going to have a Samhain (not Hallowe'en) celebration. Design a poster inviting people to this event. What would you tell them about it? How would you explain it to them?

4. Have a look at the logo of the Scottish Pagan Federation (at **www.scottishpf.org**). What does this logo say about Pagan beliefs? If you were going to design a logo for Paganism, what would it look like?

On your own

1. Are there any examples of Pagan beliefs and practices where you live? Do some research on your local area and make a display of your findings. If you have any practising Pagans where you live, perhaps you could invite them into school to discuss their beliefs.

2. Just as you did for the other festivals in this section, design and make a 'Happy Samhain' card.

3. Pagans believe that it is important to care for nature in all its forms. What things do you and others in your class do (or not do) to care for nature? Are there any local areas where nature could use some help?

Philosophical issues

5

Views about life after death

Ingledoink is an alien. He has been sent to Earth to find out what humans think about one of the Universe's big questions: what happens to you after you die? On his return he makes his usual report to the Great Infected Underlings of the High Council…

Oh Great Infected Underlings, I bring you greetings yet again from Ziggly 3 – which they call Earth. They have as many beliefs about the afterlife as they have reality TV programmes – and that is indeed saying something.

Firstly there are those who believe that there is a supernatural dwelling-place that your spirit goes to at the end of your physical body's existence. This place has various names, but there are two versions of it. The first is a pleasant place full of nice things and is run by angels. You may learn the harp there and spend your days floating around on clouds. The other possibility is that you go to a scary place that is full of bonfires and forks – but the things they'll be grilling are the people who've been sent there. These people are there because they have been bad in their lives. It seems that they stay there forever. There is a third option called Limbo – where you either try to get under very low barriers or hang around trying to avoid the bad place and end up in the good one.

Others believe that after death you wait. Then at the end of time your physical body is raised and you are judged. After this judgement, you can end up in one of the two places I mentioned already. The tricky thing is that many humans get their bodies burned after death – so what harm the fiery pits of Hell could do to a pile of ashes I'm not at all sure.

Then there are those who believe that you have something called a soul. This is a non-physical entity that exists inside you, (but not like the parasitic worms of the Arlonaterx galaxy). This soul passes on into another body and has another life – perhaps millions of lives. You might go from human to chicken to human again, provided you were a very good chicken. At the end of all this is another special place, called Nirvana. Others believe that you don't have a soul, but that you do live again in another physical body. But you don't seem to remember anything of this old life in your new life.

In all of these beliefs, there is the idea that what happens after death is linked to what you did in life. But some humans seem to have very short lives and so wouldn't have much time to be very good or bad – what happens to them isn't clear at all. Others think that what happens after death is nothing to do with whether you're good or bad but whether you believe the right things or not. But again, some humans don't have time to have any beliefs before they die, and others live long lives without being able to think very much at all.

Finally, there are those who believe that death is the end. All that you were is gone and will never return – but they still hope to 'live on' in the hearts and minds of other people, so it's not as simple as it first seemed.

Some believe that you can speak with the dead; others believe that they have seen them; others believe that they have lived before. All in all, this is probably one of the most complicated beliefs these humans have, but then it is an issue across the whole Universe…

Life after death

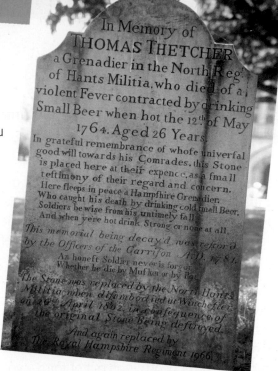

Ingledoink has found out that humans have many different beliefs about life after death. The beliefs you have are probably related very closely to the views of your parents and the time and place in which you live. In some places, the dead are honoured and treated very much as if they are still around. In other places, the dead are thought of as in another place – somewhere the living can't contact them. Many also believe that the dead are completely gone and have no existence of any kind. Humans have something that – as far as we know – no other living thing has: a sense of self-awareness. This means that we can think of the past as well as imagine the future. This is generally a good thing but it causes one major problem: we all know that one day we will die. There's nothing we can do about it. This makes us ask questions about what might happen to 'us' afterwards. It can also make us ask how the life we live now might influence what comes next.

Active Learning

1. Do some research in your class and school. What beliefs are there about life after death? Design a questionnaire – which should be strictly confidential – and report on your findings using tables, graphs and displays. Ask not only what people believe about life after death but also why they believe it.

2. Once you have completed this task you could write an illustrated article for a teen magazine or the school magazine, if you have one.

3. Create a piece of artwork that expresses your views on life after death.

4. Invite a variety of people into school to discuss their views about life after death. Alternatively, you could find many different views by Googling 'views about life after death'. You could then take on the role of someone with particular beliefs, and express the view they would have if they came to your class.

5. Gravestones often have words that express beliefs about life after death, or statues or images that express beliefs. Have a look at some gravestones – what different beliefs are expressed? Again, if this is not possible you could look at gravestones on the web. One site that gives ideas for gravestone inscriptions is **www.buzzle.com/articles/ideas-for-headstone-inscriptions.html**

Talking and listening

- What do you believe happens after death? Why do you believe this?
- What different beliefs are there in your class and community about this issue?
- Does it matter what our beliefs about life after death are?
- If you believe in life after death, how is your next life 'decided'?
- If you don't believe in life after death, what do you think is the point of your (brief) life?

1. Choose one of the beliefs about life after death. Write your own explanation of what this belief is and which belief system it is linked to.

2. In the first unit (Beliefs), you looked at a variety of different religious and non-religious views. Choose three religions (or two and a non-religious viewpoint). Now write down some beliefs about life after death on small cards, and match these belief cards with the religions they are linked to.

3. Here are two statements about life after death. Explain which one you agree with more and why.
   a. 'There is no evidence for life after death so it makes no sense to believe in it.'
   b. 'Believing in life after death is an act of faith – you don't need evidence for faith.'

4. Imagine Ingledoink arrived in your class to interview you about your beliefs about life after death. Write a short dialogue that you might have with him.

On your own

1. This topic is not one most young people discuss with their parents after a certain age. Discuss your beliefs with your parents – there's no need to report this back to class.

2. People's beliefs about life after death are often reflected in what they say and do at funerals. In what different ways are funerals carried out across Scotland and the world? An Internet search would be useful here.

3. Life after death is a popular topic for the movies. Find out how one movie treats life after death and write a short report about this.

It's a wonderful afterlife.

Reese Witherspoon   Mark Ruffalo

Just Like Heaven

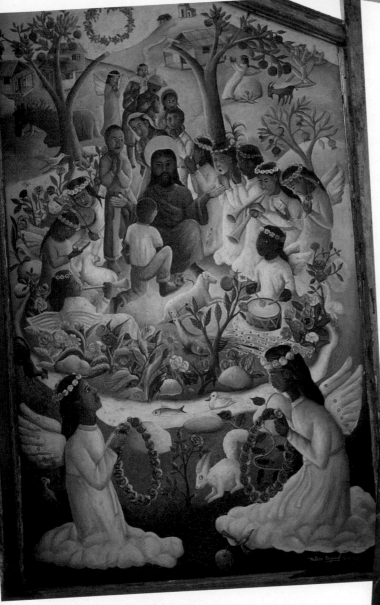

![talking and listening icon] **Talking and listening**

- What does the painting of Heaven suggest about the kind of place it is?
- What does the painting of Hell suggest about the kind of place it is?
- Do you believe in a Heaven or a Hell?
- Do you think believing in a Heaven or a Hell is a helpful thing for people? How might it affect their lives?
- Why do some people believe in Heaven and Hell and some do not?

Heaven and Hell

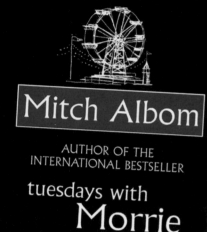

Many Christians believe that after death your soul is sent to Heaven or Hell. Heaven is pictured as a perfect place where everything is joyful and happy. In the past, Christians saw Heaven as a place in the sky, cloudy and filled with angels – and Hell as beneath the Earth, fiery and full of evil demons. Nowadays, many Christians simply believe that Heaven is where you are in God's presence for the rest of eternity. Hell, on the other hand, is a place of eternal torment and punishment. Here, God is definitely not present and his absence is part of the punishment. Many Christians believe that whether you go to Heaven or Hell depends on whether you have been good or bad in your life. However, many Christians also believe that whether you go to Heaven or Hell depends on whether you believe in God or not. Both last for all eternity and there doesn't seem to be any way to move from one to the other.

Jewish people also believe in Heaven (Gan Eden) and Hell (Gehenom/She'ol), although there's some disagreement here. One view is that wicked people end up in She'ol and stay there for nearly a year of punishment – after which either their soul is completely destroyed or they are allowed entry to Gan Eden. However, most Jewish teachers say that it is more important to focus on life now than to worry about the afterlife. In Islam there is also a belief in Heaven and Hell. All of these faiths believe that God is merciful and kind, so there are disagreements about whether he would punish someone for all eternity or not. What do you think?

Active Learning

1. Design your own piece of artwork depicting your idea of Heaven or Hell.

2. Choose a piece of music that would be suitable to go with each of the two pictures on page 69. Explain your choice of music. Listen to some examples in class – whose music is the most suitable for each picture? Why?

3. There is a book called *The Five People You Meet in Heaven*. In this book, the main character meets five people who help him understand the life he has lived. These are all people he has had something to do with in life. Who would your five people be? What would they teach you about your life?

4. For some people, Heaven is the best things you can imagine; Hell is the worst things. Create a class display where people complete the sentences: 'Heaven is…' and 'Hell is…'

5. Find out more about the similarities and differences between Jewish, Christian and Muslim beliefs about Heaven. Prepare a short project on your findings.

On your own

1. Many ancient and modern works of art have Heaven and/or Hell as their subject. Find some examples of these. How closely do they match the ideas of Heaven and Hell you have studied in this section?

2. According to many religious people, Heaven is filled with angels and Hell with demons. What are these creatures? What do people believe about them?

3. How many people in your class believe in the existence of a soul? What explanations do they give for their beliefs?

Progress Check

1. Discuss this statement in class and decide what your views on it are: 'There can be no such thing as Hell if there is such a thing as a loving God.' Try to think about how someone might argue in favour of this statement or against it.

2. Think of some well-known world baddies. If they decided just before they died that they'd lived a bad life and asked God to forgive them for it, would they end up in Heaven? Discuss in class.

3. Here are some further statements about Heaven and Hell for discussion. Choose one that you strongly agree with one that you strongly disagree with, and for each of them say why.
   a. 'Heaven just sounds boring.'
   b. 'Heaven and Hell are just fairy stories.'
   c. 'Believing in Heaven and Hell makes no difference in your life.'
   d. 'Believing in Heaven and Hell can change your life.'
   e. 'If you don't believe in Heaven you'll go to Hell.'
   f. 'There will only be good people in Heaven.'
   g. 'Only religious people can go to Heaven.'
   h. 'Heaven is just wishful thinking.'
   i. 'Hell is just a scary story to make you be good in life.'

4. Make up a short quiz on Heaven and Hell – or design a board game where the aim is to get to Heaven or avoid going to Hell.

23 Judgement Day

Yes, it's the game for all the family, and we mean all the family – right back to the first human ancestor! ANYONE can play – in fact they have to! DEAD? No worries – you'll be brought back to LIFE to play this game! You could be a SHEEP or a GOAT – or maybe you'll be one of the lucky ones to be WHEAT – but watch out for that CHAFF and just pray it's NOT YOU!

Marvel at the GREAT BOOK at the very heart of the game – every thing you have ever done is in there/… yes, EVERYTHING … there's nowhere to hide, nowhere to run; listen as it's all read out in front of everyone who ever lived! Watch your friends and family's horrified faces as they hear of your most embarrassing thoughts and actions! CRINGE at the memories of things you'd tried to forget doing! It's there for all to see! Did you feed the hungry? Did you visit the sick? NO? Then it's all coming back your way and you really don't want it to.

Cower from the brightness of the SHINING WHITE THRONE – lighting all your wicked thoughts and actions up! See those ANGELS pointing at you and laughing out loud! Watch the WINNOWING! Gaze at the THRESHING! And listen to the WAILING and the GNASHING of TEETH! Got no teeth? Worry not: TEETH WILL BE PROVIDED.

At the end of the game the winners are those who get to the RIGHT HAND. Those who only make it to the left are DOOMED for all time. And at the end of the game, bask in the glow of the ETERNAL FIRE OF PUNISHMENT … or maybe IN the eternal fire of punishment! Experience the UTTER DESTRUCTION of your SOUL – and there's no 'get out of Hell free' card here!

Buy JUDGEMENT DAY today! And get ready to play – because whether you like it or not, it's coming to you… sooner than you think!

JUDGEMENT DAY… it'll be the last game you ever play.

(Optional extras include Messianic version and Salvation by Faith version.)

(Also available in some countries as QIYAMAH, with unique features such as standing on the plains of Arafat.)

🗨 Talking and listening

■ If everything you had ever thought, said or done was to be written in a book, how would you feel about this book being read out to everyone?

■ Do you think your bad thoughts, words and actions would outweigh your good ones?

■ If Judgement Day is true, what do you think might happen to all the souls/bodies of everyone who has ever lived between their death and their being brought back to life?

■ What do you think of the idea of a Judgement Day?

Judgement Day

Many Christians believe that at the end of time, Jesus will return and bring everyone who has ever lived back to life. They will then be judged on their actions in life. If the bad actions outweigh the good, then they will be thrown into a fire of eternal punishment. If it's the other way around then they get to live in the presence of God for ever more. Many Eastern Orthodox Churches have a wall with artwork that illustrates belief in a Judgement Day. It is there to remind you about what is likely to happen at the end of time, but also to remind you that how you live your life is important.

However, there are many views about Judgement Day in Christianity. Many Christians think that it is actually going to happen; others say that you are judged at the end of your life, not on one day at the end of time. Of course, as you know, many think that eternal punishment or reward are not linked to your actions but to whether or not you believe in God.

In Islam, there is a belief that everyone will stand before God on a day known as Qiyamah. Here, your life will be judged and you will be treated accordingly. However, Muslims also believe that God is merciful and will show forgiveness to you on that day. In Judaism, before Judgement Day the Messiah will come and there will be many signs that Judgement Day is just around the corner.

Active Learning

1. Create your own artwork depicting what you have learned about Judgement Day. You could also choose some music to go with your artwork that matches its mood.

2. Many Jewish people believe that the Messiah will come before Judgement Day. What is meant by the Messiah? Do your own research and report your findings.

3. Find out if anyone you know believes in a Judgement Day. What do they believe? Why do they believe this? How does it affect their life? (You will find that even within one religion there are many different views about Judgement Day.)

4. Don't go into too much detail here, but what would your Judgement Day book look like at the moment?

5. Imagine a computer games developer was given the task of making a 'Judgement Day' game. What kind of features would it have?

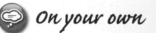
1. Whether you have done number four above or not, try this out. You will want to keep this confidential (in fact, after you've done it you'll probably want to chuck it away!). Keep a Judgement Day diary for a day. In this, record all your good thoughts, words and action and all your bad ones. At then end of the day work out how your good and bad things balance up for the day. Does recording this information make you more or less likely to do things you shouldn't?

2. Give your life so far 'two stars and a wish'. The two stars are for things you have done that are really good and the wish is something you'd rather not have done. Again, you'll probably want to keep this to yourself.

3. Just like the idea of Hell, many people – including religious people – think that the idea of Judgement Day can't be true because it doesn't match up with their belief in a God who is kind and loving. Discuss this in class. Is Judgement Day just a way to scare people into being good? Does it help you think about your actions in life?

4. Look at the Judgement Day artwork in this section. Describe what it tells you about beliefs about Judgement Day.

On your own

1. Find other examples of artwork depicting Judgement Day. What different things do they focus on? What is each artist trying to express?

2. Use the letters of the phrase 'Judgement Day' to create an acrostic that explains this belief.

3. Carry out a brief survey into how much people know about Judgement Day. Is this idea still widely believed in your community?

Ingledoink the alien is back again. This time he's been sent to Earth to find out about humans' beliefs about reincarnation. He gets to interview both a Buddhist monk, Amforashandi, and a Hindu holy man, Nigel. Of course he can't just appear in front of them, so he has carried out this interview by getting into their heads when they are meditating…

Ingledoink: So, Nigel – tell me about reincarnation.

Nigel: It's very simple really. Each person has an atman – a spiritual self. Some call it a soul. It is attached to this body as long as it lives, and then when the body dies the atman moves into another physical body.

Ingledoink: Another human?

Nigel: Perhaps. But it depends on your karma. You see, throughout your life you can build up good karma or bad karma. This is a kind of score you attract for the things you say, or do, or think. If in this life you live in a particular way, then the next life will be linked to that previous lifestyle – like if you are really sneaky in this life you'll come back as a sneaky animal or thing.

Ingledoink: Does your atman go on forever?

Nigel: You can be reincarnated millions of times until you get it right. Then you hit the jackpot and get Moksha – release from the endless cycle of birth and rebirth; becoming one with God, like a drop of water returning to the ocean.

Ingledoink: Hang on Nigel, I've got someone on the other line. Amforashandi, can you hear me?

Amforashandi: Yes I can, but I'm not all that used to people having conversations in my head in the middle of meditation.

Ingledoink: Yes, sorry about that. You heard what Nigel said?

Amforashandi: Hard not to. I agree with a lot of what Nigel said, but there are some differences too. We Buddhists don't believe in the atman or soul, but we do think that your kamma builds up through your life (I don't know where we lost the 'r' or why, by the way) and decides what your rebirth will be like.

Ingledoink: So if you haven't got an atman, what goes into the next rebirth?

Amforashandi: A kind of pattern. You're made up of different elements called skandhas. These are shaped by the life you live. Each second decides what you will be the next second, so you're kind of reborn all the time. At the end of your physical life your pattern of skandhas moves into a new physical form – which could be anything.

Ingledoink: And do you aim for Moksha too?

Amforashandi: Technically speaking we don't aim for anything, but our idea of Nibbana is a very similar idea to Moksha.

Ingledoink: Sorry guys, there's someone at the holographic portal. I have to go now…

Reincarnation and rebirth

If there is such a thing as an atman, then why are 'you' not aware of it? Are such 'spiritual' things real? Hindus believe that the soul moves through countless lives in an almost endless cycle of birth and rebirth. How can you 'learn' to build up good karma and avoid bad karma if you aren't even aware of your own atman? Also, what things count as good and bad karma? Is killing one person less bad karma than killing ten? If you're reborn as an ant, how do you build up good karma to be reborn as a human again? If you are reborn every second then do you actually exist at all? Some Hindus and Buddhists say that some people can remember their previous lives. When an important holy person dies, like a high Lama, monks go off in search of his reborn self. They believe that this person will recognise things about his past life (this is what happened with the Dalai Lama). In both Hinduism and Buddhism, the final goal is release from rebirth and so the absolute end of anything that can be described as 'you'. What do you think?

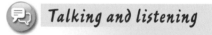

Active Learning

1. Have a look at the Tibetan Buddhist wheel of life on page 77. This separates our countless lives into realms and groups. Find out what these are. You could draw your own version of this wheel and explain what's going on in each section.

2. Illustrate the five skandhas of Buddhism. They are: solid form; feelings and physical sensations; experiences (like seeing and hearing things); will (doing things); and consciousness (or mental awareness).

3. Create a collage of images on a display board showing what might be good and bad karma/kamma.

4. Think about good and bad actions. Give them a good or bad rating. Are some actions much better or worse than others? Why? What agreements and disagreements are there about this in your class?

5. Some people believe that there is scientific evidence for the idea of a past life. They claim that during hypnosis, people remember things from a previous life. Find out more about this and discuss it in class. What are your views?

Talking and listening

- What do you think of the idea of reincarnation/rebirth?
- Do you believe in the existence of an atman/soul?
- If reincarnation/rebirth is true why don't we have any memories of our past lives?
- What do you think would be good karma/kamma and bad?
- How much good and bad karma/kamma do you have right now?

1. In your own words, explain the meaning of the following words: karma; reincarnation; rebirth; skandhas; atman; Moksha; Nibbana.

2. Here are some statements about reincarnation and rebirth to discuss in class. Which ones do you agree with and which do you disagree with? Explain your views.
   a. 'Reincarnation and rebirth are just ideas to make you behave well in life.'
   b. 'Reincarnation and rebirth are just wishful thinking.'
   c. 'Reincarnation and rebirth are just ideas to stop you being afraid of death.'
   d. 'There's no point in believing in Moksha and Nibbana because there's no evidence for them.'
   e. 'If you'd lived before, you'd remember something about it.'
   f. 'Reincarnation is a more helpful belief than Heaven/Hell or Judgement Day.'

3. Look back at your Judgement Day diary page from the previous section. How's your karma/kamma doing today?

4. Create a pie chart of views in your class as follows:
   a. people who believe in Heaven and Hell
   b. people who believe in Judgement Day
   c. people who believe in reincarnation/rebirth
   d. people who don't know what they believe about life after death
   e. people who believe that there is nothing after death.

 **On your own**

1. Go to Google Images and type in the words below. What images appear? Choose one image for each word and turn this into a PowerPoint display for your class.
   Words: reincarnation; rebirth; Moksha; Nibbana; atman; soul; skandha.

2. As before, interview friends and family about reincarnation/rebirth. What different views are held?

3. The Bloxham Tapes are interviews with people who, under hypnosis, seemed to remember past lives. Find out more about this 'evidence'. What do its supporters say about it? How have people challenged it?

My name is Ken and all my life I've been a Humanist
So I reject religion and all the gods they list
They say that life's not over when your body's time is done
And off you go to Heaven, which really doesn't sound like fun
Or maybe you end up in Hell where you are boiled and roasted
And your fingers, toes and eyeballs are all without mercy toasted
Or maybe get the chance to write again your whole life's story
Through putting right your nasty wrongs in that place called
   purgatory
The whole thing seems quite strange to me – in fact it's very odd
That such endless punishment could come from a loving God
And then there's all that weirdy stuff about your mortal soul
Which has annihilation as its last and final goal
Your atman will attain release from the endless rounds of birth
And death as well, though Moksha also sounds devoid of mirth
And then there's those five skandhas of which we're supposedly made
Which means we're reborn all the time and our new self conveyed
Into another body where our pattern takes its form
You might be a chicken or a duck or a man with a beard called Norm
So what do I think?
I think that when you're dead, you're gone – never to return
Bury your body, or burn it up and place what's left in an urn
For nothing comes along after death just like nothing came before
There is no Heaven, Hell, rebirth or supernatural door
I hear you say: 'But aren't you sad when you think there's nothing after death?'
No, indeed I'm not, and I'll say so even with my final breath
For what you do *in this life* is what matters most to me
And not what could come afterwards – there's no evidence, you see
I live the fullest life I can, enjoy it and have fun
That's even more important when you think there's only one
Through music, science, art and love – and all the best in life
And helping others do so too, avoiding pain and strife
Our values, morality, purpose in life: these aren't things I lose
I find them in other people, and taking responsibility in what I *choose*
So I may live on after death but not in spiritual parts
But rather in story, memories, achievements, minds and hearts

BRITISH HUMANIST ASSOCIATION
for the one life we have

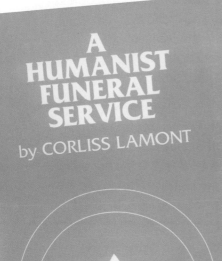

Talking and listening

- How many people in your class believe that death is the end and that there's nothing afterwards?
- Why might some people find the belief that death is the end quite sad? What do you think?
- Do you live life to the fullest, as if it is your only one?
- If there's no Heaven / Hell / Judgement Day / karma / kamma, does that mean people won't worry about being good?
- What things in life make it worth living for you?

A
HUMANIST
FUNERAL
SERVICE
by CORLISS LAMONT

Humanist view

Humanists don't believe that to be important and valued people must have a soul, or to be made 'in the image of God'. These supernatural and divine things are actually a distraction from what really matters, they say. Humanists think that people are valuable in themselves, because of who they are and what they mean to each other. Humanists don't believe that God gave us responsibility to look after one another. Instead our moral responsibility is something that we must choose to take upon ourselves, and for a humanist this makes it all the more valuable and all the more a *moral* choice.

Humanists do not accept religion. They think that all the things we believe should be backed up by evidence, and they don't find any evidence to support the claims of religion or any kind of life after death. Humanists believe that when you die, that is the end. They see this as a perfectly positive belief because it means that they value the one life they have very highly. Also, Humanists believe that you should live this life in the best way you can – causing no harm to others and helping people get the most out of their lives. Humanists don't do this so they can get some kind of reward after death – they do it because they think it makes the world a better place. Humanists believe that we have to sort out the problems in the world ourselves because there is no God to do it for us. What do you think of the Humanist view?

Active Learning

1. Find out about basic Humanist views and design an information poster about them. You can find loads of information at www. humanism-scotland.org.uk.

2. Famous Humanists include scientists such as Richard Dawkins, Gene Roddenberry (the creator of *Star Trek*) and the author Terry Pratchett. You can find many more simply by typing 'famous Humanists' into any search engine. Create fact files or displays about these famous Humanists.

3. Just as religious funerals reflect religious beliefs about the afterlife, humanist funerals reflect the view that there is no afterlife. Carry out some further research into religious and non-religious funeral practices. How do these practices reflect beliefs?

4. Write a script or dialogue where Ingledoink the alien (from chapters 21 and 24) tries to find out about Humanist views on life after death.

5. Go back to your pie chart in Chapter 24. Now find a couple of people who said that they did not believe in anything after death. Why do they believe this? How does it affect their life (if at all)? You could interview them and film it as if you were doing a TV chat show.

1. Here are two opposite statements about Humanist views on life after death. Have a debate in which one half of the class supports each view.
   a. 'The Humanist view that there is nothing after death is quite depressing and means you can live your life however you want.'
   b. 'The Humanist view that there is nothing after death is a positive view that means that you're even more careful about how you live this life.'

2. Create a piece of artwork illustrating the Humanist view of death. Given that they don't believe in an afterlife, you might like to focus on the ideas expressed in the last line of the poem at the start of this Chapter.

3. Humanists say that the things we do make life precious, not the hope of an afterlife. Create your own multimedia display exploring the things that make life worth living.

4. Copy and complete your own summary table of the topics you have looked at in this Unit:

Religion/ viewpoint	Beliefs/views about life after death	What I think about this
Christianity		
Judaism		
Islam		
Hinduism		
Buddhism		
Humanism		

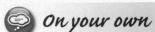

1. Write your own personal reflection on this Unit using the following headings:
   a. new things I have learned about beliefs about life after death
   b. how my own views about life after death have changed
   c. something I found out in this section that surprised me.

2. Choose one religious group – perhaps one you have studied in some other setting – and find out more about their beliefs on life after death. This could be from a different part of the world or a different period in time. Some ideas are:
   a. the Vikings
   b. the ancient Greeks
   c. the Aboriginal people of Australia
   d. the Inuit
   e. Pacific peoples
   f. Bahai.

3. Using the information in this Unit, create a short test about life after death. This should test knowledge and get people to reflect upon what they have learned too.

6

The rights of animals

School cafeteria, Monday lunchtime. Ricky and Nicky sit down to lunch. Ricky bites into his succulent cheeseburger…

Nicky: Mooo! Mooo! MOOO!

Ricky: [*Coughing and spluttering*] What's with you and the mooing?

Nicky: Just reminding you what you're eating.

Ricky: I'm eating a burger.

Nicky: You're eating a cow – or maybe a little calf, all wide-eyed and soppy, snuggling up to its mummy before they shipped it off down the slaughterhouse, shot it through the head with a zillion volts, boiled it, skinned it, minced it and stuck it in your burger bap.

Ricky: Aw come on, eating meat is perfectly natural. We've got canine teeth so that we can tear meat.

Nicky: Just because humans ate meat in the past doesn't mean they have to eat meat now. If you had to kill the animal, skin it and cook it before you ate it, would you?

Ricky: Probably… if I had to.

Nicky: Aye right. You can't see the link between what you're eating and the little life form it used to be attached to.

Ricky: Look, the animal would never have existed in the first place if the farmer hadn't had it born so he could sell it. And it probably had quite a nice life.

Nicky: Know that for a fact, do you? Anyway, do you think it's ok to give something a life just so you can kill it a few years later?

Ricky: It's only an animal.

Nicky: So are humans. You think it's ok to kill animals for food just because they can't tell us they'd rather not be eaten?

Ricky: So… what are you saying here Nicky?

Nicky: [*Slowly and loudly*] STOP EATING MEAT!

Ricky: I don't see why I should.

Nicky: I give up, I really do…

Talking and listening

- Do you eat meat? Why? Why not?
- Do you think most people would eat meat if they had to kill the animal themselves?
- Would animals volunteer to be slaughtered?
- Is meat-eating perfectly natural?
- Is it ok to eat some animals but not others?

Animals as food

Dogs, cats, rats, guinea pigs, insects. These are just some of the animals eaten around the world. Why is eating these any different from eating cows, pigs and chickens as we do in Scotland? Some people say that eating meat is a natural thing for humans to do. Besides, as long as the animal was treated well during its life and killed with as little pain as possible, then what's the problem? Other people argue that eating meat is a cruel misuse of human power over the animal world. Also, they say that we don't need to eat meat because producing it is environmentally wasteful and, most importantly, unnecessary – humans can meet all their nutritional needs without meat. Some say that the conditions animals are kept in before they are slaughtered are very cruel. You probably buy most of your meat from a butcher or supermarket, so it's hard to make the link between the animal and the meat on your plate. Is this just the way things are, or are people not facing up to what they're really doing? Is meat-eating natural, or is it pointless cruelty?

 Active Learning

1. List as many animals as you can think of on small pieces of card. Post them up on a board under two headings: 'I would eat this' and 'I would not eat this'. Invite people to move the cards around according to their views. Afterwards, find out which of the animals on your board are eaten around the world and which are not. (The Vegetarian Society has an interesting article about this called 'The butcher's cat' – **www.butcherscat.com**.)

2. Some people say that the problem is how the animals are treated before slaughter. Find out about the following practices and design information sheets about each one: battery chickens; intensive pig farming; farrowing stalls; veal crates; free-range chickens; organic farming; intensive turkey rearing for Christmas; fish farming. You should try to present a balanced picture, showing arguments for and against.

3. Others say that killing an animal is wrong, no matter how it has been treated. Script a dialogue between you and Eric the Turkey where Eric – now magically able to speak – expresses his views on being Christmas dinner.

4. Some people say that eating meat is nutritionally unnecessary. Find out about the evidence they use to support this view. Prepare a short report on the nutritional requirements of someone your age, and the extent to which they can be satisfied without meat. The Vegetarian Society website (**www.vegsoc.org**) should help you here (go to the 'Young Veggie' section). Balance this up by looking at the Quality Meat Scotland website (**www.qmscotland.co.uk**).

5. Work with your Home Economics department to design a nutritionally balanced vegetarian or vegan meal.

1. The philosopher Peter Singer says that if you eat meat then you are a 'speciesist'. This means that you discriminate against animals based on the fact that they are a different species to you. He thinks this is no better than sexism or racism. Write your views on this – are meat-eaters guilty of discrimination?

2. Here is a series of statements about meat-eating. For each one, say whether you agree or disagree and explain your answer.
   a. 'If we eat animals we might as well eat humans too.'
   b. 'Using animals to make leather goods and fur coats is no different to eating them.'
   c. 'It's ok to eat an animal, but only if you hunt and kill it yourself.'
   d. 'Some people in the world don't have a choice – they have to eat animals.'
   e. 'We can eat some animals but not others.'

3. Do some research in your class/school and produce two pie charts. One could look at whether pupils (and staff) in your school are meat-eaters, vegetarians or vegans. The other could look at whether people would like to be meat-eaters, vegetarians or vegans. Is there any difference between what people are and what they would like to be?

4. The Indian leader Mahatma Gandhi said that the worth of a society is judged by how it treats its animals. Have a class debate about one of the issues linked to meat-eating, and have a vote at the end.

 On your own

1. The haggis is Scotland's traditional dish. Find out what's in it and think about whether its contents are gross or a good use of meat. (You can of course get veggie haggis too.)

2. If you are a meat-eater, you could try a week without meat. If you're already a veggie you could try being a vegan. How do you feel at the end of the week? If you're a vegan, look more closely at some of the labels on the products you eat – are there any surprises?

Man in street 1: It's disgusting, the things they still do to animals in the twenty-first century. And all so that we can look or smell pretty! Let's say you want to test some mascara – you get some poor little rabbit and you drop this stuff into its eye until its eyeball is burned out. But who cares – it's just a little bunny after all.

Spokesman for 'Lush Lashes' mascara company: Yes, I know it looks a little… well… cruel, but I'm afraid we have to do these things. But you could hardly expect people to use a product, especially near their eyes, that might do them damage. So, yes, we might use animals to test the product, but we could hardly use humans, could we?

Man in street 2: Ok, so when I've got a headache I'll take a pill – but I didn't expect that pill to be tested on some poor animal. You can get human volunteers for that kind of thing, can't you? Or couldn't you use some artificial skin or a computer program or something? Besides, just because it didn't do the animal any harm how do I know it's not going to do me any harm? We can't ask the animals for permission to use them, so should we use them? I wouldn't like people to force me to test out a new drug.

Spokesman from 'Douggie's Drugs' pharmaceutical company: We need to make sure our pills are safe, and we can't take chances with people's lives by getting them to try out new drugs that could have terrible side-effects. Besides, many cures we have nowadays have come about through using animals during testing. You couldn't give a human cancer just to test an anti-cancer drug, could you? But you can with a rat. And while we're at it, do you know how many rats are killed each year by vermin exterminators?

🗨 *Talking and listening*

- Should animals be used to test cosmetic items like shampoos and perfumes?
- Should animals be used to test medicines?
- Do you find out if your cosmetic products are 'cruelty-free' or not?
- Is it ok to do things to animals that we wouldn't do to people?
- Which products are usually tested on animals?

Animal experimentation

When a company makes a product, they have to show that it is safe for human use. This often involves testing the product on animals. In Europe there are strict laws about the use of animals to test cosmetics, but in some countries these laws are not as strict. Some cosmetics are not tested on animals – they might have a 'cruelty-free' or 'not tested on animals' label displayed on them. The Body Shop was one of the first retailers to make cruelty-free products big business. All sorts of other household items are tested on animals, such as furniture polish and toilet cleaners. Testing medicines on animals is still more common than cosmetic testing. Animals are used in scientific research to test out new cures for all sorts of illnesses and diseases. Some people say that there is no safe alternative to using an animal; others disagree. However, many cures for illness and disease have come through animal testing, but many mistakes have also been made. What do you think about the use of animals in experiments?

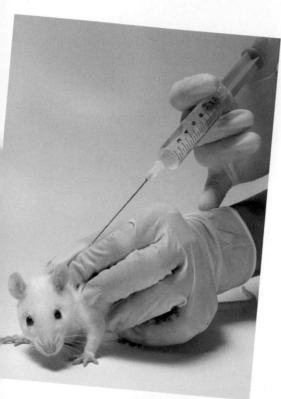

Active Learning

1. Set up a display in your classroom of common cosmetic products (get people to bring them in from home). Sort them into either 'tested on animals' or 'not'. Products that have not been tested on animals usually say so clearly on the labels. If you're not sure, go to the website for the product and try to find out. How many products are animal-tested and how many are not? (You can find a list of cruelty-free cosmetic producers at **www.gocrueltyfree. org/e_retailers.php**.)

2. What medical experiments are carried out on animals? What alternatives are possible? What are the arguments for and against? Prepare a short illustrated project on this topic. You should try to make your project as balanced as possible. Here are some websites that could help.

In favour of using animals in scientific research	Opposed to using animals in scientific research
www.pro-test.org.uk	www.buav.org
www.understandinganimalresearch.org.uk	www.uncaged.co.uk
www.animalresearch.info/en/home	www.animalaid.org.uk

BUAV approved

3. Create an exhibition covering animal experimentation issues. Again, try to keep the argument as balanced as possible. Include images and written information. (Be sensitive in your use of images, though.)

4. Now think about your own views. Are you a supporter of using animals in experiments or not? Choose either cosmetic testing or scientific/medical research and design a campaign poster either for or against the use of animals in this kind of research. No need to be balanced here!

5. Write a letter to your MSP expressing your views on the treatment of animals in experimentation. It's up to you whether your letter is supporting animal experimentation or not.

Progress Check

1. In groups, summarise the arguments for and against animal testing for cosmetic purposes and for medical purposes. See which group can come up with the most arguments for and against.

2. Look at the arguments that you have produced as a class. Now put them in order, with the strongest arguments at the top and the weakest ones at the bottom. Display your results; how 'strong' are the arguments on either side?

3. In the form of a song or poem, express your own views on the use of animals in experiments.

4. Sometimes people who oppose the use of animals in experiments protest. These can range from peaceful marches to breaking into labs and releasing animals. Find out about some of the ways in which people protest against animal experiments. Are some protests more justifiable than others?

On your own

1. Carry out your own survey on people's views about animal experimentation and report on your findings.

2. Decide what your views on animal experimentation are. Now design a front page for your own website that explains your views.

3. Imagine Ingledoink the alien (from chapters 21 and 24) arrived and quizzed you about the use of animals on Earth today. Script the conversation that you might have.

Polly: Wings? Yeah sure I've got wings. What did you expect? Not much call for them in here though. Hop from one perch to another… then hop back to the other one again. I could do it all day. In fact, I do do it all day! Well, there's nothing else to do in here, is there? Oh, I do have a mirror, and it's got a bell too. I know, I can barely contain myself with the sheer joy of it all: a mirror – and a bell – too much! Yes, I do need to get out more. But that's hardly likely to be the case is it…

Ralph: It's embarrassing. I mean, out we go and I'm doing my personal business… you know… and they're just standing watching. Then what do they say? 'Good boy, well done' like I'm a complete idiot. What was I supposed to do instead? Hold it in until I explode and fire it all over the house? I don't think so. And then there's the food. Is it prime venison right off the back of a freshly killed deer? No such luck. Pellets… little hard wormy-like solid pellets of dust mixed with who knows what. Either that or some unspeakable gunk out of a tin – some kind of jellied rabbit brains. Pure boggin', it is.

Dexter: Running about? Meeting up with my chums? Not much chance of that in here I'll tell you… seeing as I'm in solitary confinement and all. Oh, I do have a wheel that I can run around in all day if I like – big deal. They obviously think I'm that stupid that I don't know I'm not going anywhere. Home is a plastic tray and a cage on top – too hot in summer, too cold in winter. And my sleeping quarters aren't exactly your dream crib either – a little plastic bowl made up to look like a little house. Some life, eh?

 Talking and listening

- Do you have any pets? Why do you have them?
- Do you think you treat your pets well? How do you know if you do or don't?
- Is it ok to keep any animal as a pet?
- What might your pet say to you if it could talk?
- Is keeping a pet like keeping an animal in prison?

Animals as pets

Why do so many people keep pets? Some like the company, particularly if they're elderly or live alone. Some keep pets to help their children learn about animals and the cycle of life. Some don't know why they keep pets – they just like to. Pet owners might say that their pets have a better life than they would have in the wild, and of course they might be right. But what right does anyone have to keep an animal as a pet? The animal may be far from its natural environment. It may not be able to behave the way it would naturally. It might not be able to hunt, or find a mate, or make baby animals. When we take a human away from their home and lock them up it's because they've done something bad. But we do this to millions of pets all every day – and they've done nothing wrong. Are we treating them like prisoners? Is that fair?

Active Learning

1. Find out how many people in your class/school keep pets. What kinds of pets are kept? What are they kept in? What do they do all day? What are they fed? Make a display of your findings.

2. Choose one animal that is kept as a pet. It can either be a common family pet or something more exotic. Find out about the environment in which this animal would live in the wild. How would it behave in the wild? With some animals you might need to look at their closest relatives because they've changed so much compared to how they were in the wild – for example dogs and wolves. Create a visual display split into two sections: 'in captivity' / 'in the wild'.

3. Choose an animal that is commonly kept as a pet. Ideally you should choose one that you have at home. How could you improve its life so that its experience is closer to the one it might have in the wild? Could you design more 'natural' housing for it, or treat it differently?

4. Providing pets for people is big business. Sometimes people do things that can be harmful for either the animals themselves or their natural habitat in ensuring a supply of pets for the home. Look into one of the following topics and create your own illustrated fact file about it:
    a. puppy farms (see **www.dogstrust.org.uk/az/p/ puppyfarming/default.aspx**)
    b. taking animals out of their natural environment (for example the removal of exotic marine life for home aquariums)
    c. transporting live animals over long distances
    d. capturing endangered species to supply the exotic pets market.

5. Imagine pets could talk. How would they describe their lives? What improvements and changes might they want? Create an imaginative piece of writing exploring these ideas from the pet's point of view.

1. Here are some statements about keeping pets. Put them onto cards and pass them around the classroom. Get each person to say whether they agree or disagree with each statement and explain why.
   a. 'Keeping a pet is like keeping an animal as a slave.'
   b. 'As long as pets are well treated there's nothing wrong with having them.'
   c. 'Pets have no choice about how they are kept – that's why it's wrong.'
   d. 'You can keep a pet safe and free from harm in a house – that's more than it has in the wild, so what's the problem?'
   e. 'Pets provide valuable services for their owners and in return they are cared for – where's the harm in that?'
   f. 'Just because some people are cruel to their pets doesn't mean everyone should be banned from having them.'
   g. 'A truly kind society would have no pets.'

2. Design a campaign poster protesting about one of the issues you have explored in Active Learning task 4.

3. Some pets are kept to help people out. Visit **www.petsastherapy.org**, which uses pets to help people in different circumstances. Write a short report about what you find on the website. Is it acceptable to use animals in this way?

4. Some people keep exotic pets such as snakes and lizards. Some pets are not allowed to be kept in Scotland. Draw up a list of animals you think should definitely not be kept as pets and for each one explain why.

On your own

1. Visit the website of the Scottish SPCA (**www.scottishspca.org**). What advice does it give to pet owners? What pet abuses does it discuss? What could you do to help this organisation?

2. Draw up a set of laws that should apply to household pets. Perhaps you could contact a solicitor, who could tell you more about the law in Scotland on keeping pets. (Or see **www.scottishlaw.org.uk/lawscotland/index.html**, which provides an A–Z of Scots Law.)

3. Visit some pet shops and do some research into the kinds of animals sold, how much they're sold for and how the shop ensures that the new owners understand how to look after their pets.

Progress Check

1. Discuss these statements in class and note the views expressed – what is your conclusion about each statement and why have you reached that conclusion?
   a. 'Zoos are very different from safari parks – at least in safari parks the animals have more space to move around.'
   b. 'It's ok to keep Scottish animals captive in Scottish wildlife parks, but not animals that live in other environments, like the African savannah.'
   c. 'No matter what you call it, a zoo is still an animal prison – full of creatures serving life sentences for having done nothing wrong.'
   d. 'Zoos are a necessary evil – they help to put right some of the destruction of natural habitats caused by humans around the world.'
   e. 'Animals are much safer and happier in zoos than they would be in the wild – at least in zoos they're not going to be hunted and killed!'

2. Imagine that a protest group wants to close down a zoo near you. The zoo is working normally and following all the laws that apply to it. The animals seem well cared for. Your MSP calls at your door and asks what you think. Write the discussion that you might have with the MSP.

3. Describe how a zoo can be as animal-friendly as possible.

On your own

1. Find out which zoos are thought of as the best in the world… and which are the worst. The Good Zoo Guide (**www.goodzoos.com/about.htm**) and the World Society for the Protection of Animals (**www.wspa.org.uk**) might help here.

2. Imagine a group of aliens arrived on Earth. They are in charge of the Intergalactic Zoo and proudly inform you that they want to take 100 humans and lock them up in their zoo for the rest of their lives. Would anyone go? Would the governments of the world resist this request? Is this any different from the zoos we have? Write a story about this or just give your thoughts about it.

3. Animals are often bred in zoos so that they can be used to restock populations in the wild. Which wild habitats in the world are under threat? Why? Which animals are endangered because of this?

How do different people's beliefs affect their views on animals?

Speaker 1: I am a Christian. I do not believe that it is right to eat animals or to do experiments on them. I think Jesus would expect us to be kind to animals because he said that the strong should protect the weak.

Speaker 2: I am a Christian too. In the beginning, God put humans in charge of the whole of creation. That means that we can do what we like to animals. I'm not saying that we should be cruel to them, but it's ok to eat them, and if they help scientists find the cure for diseases then it's ok to use them in experiments.

Speaker 3: I am a Buddhist. I think we should not eat animals or do experiments on them. The Buddha said that we should show compassion to all living things. Animals are tied to the endless cycle of birth and rebirth just like us – it wouldn't be right for us to interfere in that.

Speaker 4: I am a Buddhist too. I think we should treat animals with care, but the Buddha also said that you shouldn't stick to the rules of Buddhism like a slave – you can be flexible. That means you can eat animals and experiment on them if you need to.

Speaker 5: I am a Humanist. I don't think there's anything wrong with eating animals. But humans should also act responsibly in everything they do – so that means not being cruel to animals before we eat them. I also think that it's ok to use animals in experiments. If that's the only way to find a cure, then that's what we have to do.

Speaker 6: I am a Humanist too, but I don't think we should eat animals. Killing something when you don't have to is wrong – we can get all the vitamins we need without eating meat. Also, what's the point in using animals to test cures for human diseases? Animals aren't humans, so what can we learn from them?

🗨 *Talking and listening*

- How do you think we should treat animals? Why?
- In what ways are your views about animals linked to your beliefs?
- Why do you think there are disagreements within religions and non-religious viewpoints about how we should treat animals?
- From what you know about Jesus and the Buddha already, do you think they would have eaten meat?
- Do you think that religious people and Humanists speak out about animal issues often enough?

Beliefs and animals

You should be becoming more aware that people's beliefs and views affect how they live their lives. Some Christians and Buddhists are vegetarians or vegans and some are not. In fact, many religious celebrations around the world – such as Christmas, Easter, Eid and Passover – involve having great feasts with meat as the main dish. Some faiths still ritually sacrifice animals as part of their celebrations. Many religions have particular rules about which animals can and cannot be eaten, and some have special ways of killing the animals that they say is less painful. Most religions have rules about how animals should be treated, but followers of these religions sometimes understand these rules in different ways. Because Humanists don't have holy books and rules like religions do, they try to gather the evidence for and against treating an animal in a particular way and then make up their own minds. How do your beliefs or views affect the way you think animals should be treated?

 *Active Learning*

1. Islam and Judaism have specific rules about which animals can and cannot be eaten. Find out what these rules are and display your findings. You should show which animals are halal/kosher and which are not. You should also try to find out why some animals are considered clean and some unclean to eat.

2. Link up with your Home Economics department and prepare some menus or recipes that would be ok for Muslims or Jewish people to eat. If you are Jewish or Muslim, you could help guide the non-Jews/non-Muslims in coming up with menus or recipes that would be suitable for you.

3. Many religious celebrations involve the killing and/or eating of animals. Here are some examples. Prepare an information sheet about each one, explaining what is done and why. See if you come across any religious views that are opposed to these practices:
   a. Orthodox Christianity – the roast lamb at Easter
   b. Western Christianity – Turkey at Christmas
   c. Islam – the slaughtering of animals during the annual Hajj
   d. Judaism – the presence of meat on the seder plate at Passover.

➡

On your own

1. Imagine that it is 300 years from now. Do you think that how humans treat animals will have changed? Write an imaginative story about this.

2. There are many animal issues that have not been looked at in this section. Find out about one of the following and write a short report of your findings:
   a. hunting
   b. circus acts
   c. working animals (such as guide dogs for the blind)
   d. animals in services (such as the police/army etc)
   e. animals used in sports (for example horse-racing).

3. Write a short three-wish statement about what you think you could do to act responsibly towards animals:
   a. I could…
   b. I could…
   c. I could…

4. Some people believe that not enough is said about the treatment of animals by religious and non-religious groups. Go to the following websites and find out what you can about their beliefs/views in relation to eating animals and using them in experiments.
   a. Humanism – **www.humanism-scotland.org.uk**;
   b. Christianity – Church of Scotland (**www.churchofscotland.org.uk**); see also the Science, Religion and Technology project (SRT) linked to the Church of Scotland;
   c. Christianity – the Roman Catholic Church (**www.vatican.va**)
   d. Judaism – **www.scojec.org**
   e. Islam – **www.mcscotland.org**
   f. Buddhism – **www.fwboscotland.com**.

5. Design an information leaflet for followers of one of the above faiths/viewpoints. This should get them thinking about how they should treat animals based on the teachings/arguments of their faith/viewpoint.

Progress Check

1. Explain in your own words how similar (or different) the views of religious and non-religious people are about the treatment of animals.

2. Here are some statements. Discuss them in class – do you agree or disagree?
   a. 'Religious people should be more concerned about animals than Humanists are.'
   b. 'How you treat animals has nothing to do with your beliefs or views.'

3. Some religious people say that even in their own religion, the events that involve the killing and/or eating of animals should stop. Draw up a list of arguments for and against this view.

4. What have you learned about the treatment and rights of animals in the world today? Have any of your views changed? Think about how your learning has affected your beliefs/views.

7

Exploring Christianity

A popular TV talent show. On walks a competitor. He's ordinary looking and plainly dressed, but has a certain charm. He takes up his position on stage…

Judge: Your name is?
Competitor: Joshua.
Judge: Ok Joshua, and what's your act? Are you a comedian?
Competitor: No, but I do like to make people happy.
Judge: Ok – so do you sing?
Competitor: No.
Judge: Dance?
Competitor: No.

Judge: Joshua, in case you hadn't noticed, this is a talent show… so what's your talent?
Competitor: I just thought it would make sense to appear on a show like this first – for this to be the first time people get to see me again.
Judge: *[Looking bored, annoyed and slightly confused, he asks in a mocking way…]* So you're here just to let us see you first, before you do what exactly?
Competitor: Before I put things right again.
Judge: Put what things right?
Competitor: The way things are. You see, you've all *[looks at audience too]* really let things go. You've let the world fall apart, and it needs to be healed. You don't feed the poor, you don't visit the sick, you don't comfort the prisoner. You need to look at your lives again and ask yourself some hard questions.
Judge: Right Joshua, I think that's enough. This isn't a political programme. I'm afraid you're not entertaining and you're not fun.
Competitor: But I am the way to true happiness.
Judge: NEXT! *[Judge nods to security man, who moves in to direct Joshua off the stage]*

💬 Talking and listening

- Christians believe that Jesus will return to Earth one day. Where do you think he'd make his first appearance?
- If Jesus did appear in the world today, how do you think people would react to him?
- From what you know about Jesus, what would please him or anger him about today's world?
- What things might Christians believe Jesus needs to put right?
- If Jesus met you, what might he ask you about your life?

The Jesus story: part 2

Christians believe that after his death, Jesus returned briefly to Earth and then returned to Heaven to be with his father, God. They believe he's still there. They also believe that he is spiritually present in the world today. However, they also believe that he will return to Earth one day – they call this the Second Coming. At this time, he will judge people's lives and bring in a new way of life that Christians call the Kingdom of God. Christians believe that this will be a perfect world, just the way God meant it to be in the first place, but there are disagreements about what this actually means. So, Christians say, you need to be ready: your life needs to be in order, and fit for the return of Jesus. You have to live your life like he did, by following his actions and his teachings. You need to believe in him, and think of him as the way to God. If you do all this, then you will get everlasting life, and you will join Jesus in Heaven. If Jesus returned today, what would happen next to the world and to you?

Active Learning

1. Write an imaginative story that describes the return of Jesus to Earth. How do you think he would do it? How would he look and sound? How would the world react to his arrival? Would people believe him? Might he be locked up? What would he change? Make your story as imaginative as you can and put in as much detail as possible.

2. Imagine the first place Jesus appeared was in your local community. What might he think of life round your way? Where would he go? What would he do? Who would he speak to first? Take some photos of your local community and create a display for your school with captions underneath each photo saying what Jesus might think of this – good and bad. Here are some things you might look at:
   a. What might he think of the houses people live in?
   b. What might he think of the kinds of shops there are and what they sell?
   c. What might he think of how people spend their time?
   d. What might he think of how the natural world is treated?
   e. What might he think of how Christianity is represented? (Please be sensitive about the people who live in your community, of course.)

3. Christians believe that when Jesus was here last time, many people were quite shocked about the kind of people he was friendly with. They thought he should have spent more time with the holy people – but he wasn't always impressed by them. Find out about Jesus's relationship with the following people/groups. In groups, create a fact file for one of these options, explaining Jesus's relationship to the person/group and what this tells us about the kind of person he was.
   a. Zacchaeus, the tax-collector
   b. the Roman centurion

→

c. Mary Magdalene

d. the fishermen of Galilee

e. the Pharisees

f. the traders in the temple

g. the Roman governor, Pontius Pilate

h. the rich young ruler.

4. Christians believe that Jesus taught people using parables. These were everyday stories with a message for the listeners. Choose one of the following parables and explain the story (briefly) and its meaning. Then find a newspaper article (or something from Google News) that shows where this parable could still be applied:

a. the good samaritan

b. the prodigal son

c. the widow's coin

d. the arrogant guest

e. the wise man and the foolish man

f. the talents.

 On your own

1. Many Christian organisations already try to create the Kingdom of God in Scotland. Create a short report about what they do and prepare some questions that you'd like to ask them:

a. Care for Scotland (**www.care.org.uk**)

b. Mad Ministries (**www.madinscotland.com**)

c. Bethany Christian Trust (**www.bethanychristiantrust.com**)

d. Glasgow City Mission (**www.glasgowcitymission.com**)

e. Cross Reach Scotland (**www.crossreach.org.uk**).

2. Christians believe that Jesus will come 'like a thief in the night'. Find out what they mean by this and what it means for their lives.

Progress Check

1. Christians believe that they should make the world ready for Jesus's return. What should they be doing? Organise your ideas into those which are most important and least important. You could look at your community, Scotland and the world.

2. What would Jesus think of your life today? Write down three things he'd be happy with and three changes he'd want to make. (You might want to keep this confidential.)

3. Devise a short quiz for people in your class covering what you have learned about Jesus.

A page on a fictional website called AskGod.com…

FAQs

Q: If Jesus was God's son, did God have a wife?

A: No, God created Jesus as a unique being that is part God and part human. God needs no wife for this.

Q: But if Mary was a virgin, how did she get pregnant?

A: God created the Universe and everything in it. To make a human woman pregnant but not in the usual way was therefore very simple.

Q: Why doesn't God just appear and prove he exists?

A: If he did that then you would have to believe in him – you would have no choice. God thinks it's important for you to make the choice for yourself

Q: Why did God create the devil?

A: Originally the devil was an angel, but he rejected God and so God punished him. God lets you choose whether to follow him or not.

Q: Why does God let bad things happen?

A: God has to let nature do what it does – otherwise nothing would make sense. He also has to allow people to make bad decisions and allow the consequences of their bad decisions to happen. He

doesn't like it much – but that's the way it is.

Q: Why did God let his own son be killed so horribly?

A: God allowed Jesus to make his own choices too. Jesus knew what he had to do, but God didn't force him. Jesus was trying to save everyone by turning around the mistake made by the first man, Adam.

Q: Why did God cause floods and punish people in the Bible?

A: God is like a parent – he has to teach people what's right and wrong. Sometimes this means he has to be a bit harsh.

Q: Does God have a physical body?

A: He can have, but he's most often a spiritual being.

Q: Why do people say that God is male?

A: Not everyone does. Some holy books say this so their followers say it too – some call God male and female and some just don't bother thinking about it.

Q: Will I ever get to see God?

A: Depends on how you live your life and what you believe…

Talking and listening

- Which of the questions in this discussion have you ever asked yourself?
- Which question is your 'favourite' one?
- Which answers do you agree with and which do you not agree with?
- What other questions might you ask?

God

Christians believe that God is the creator of the Universe and everything in it. They believe that he is not created, he has just always existed. Some think he has a physical form and others don't. Christians believe he is omnipotent – this means he can do anything. They believe he's omniscient – he knows everything and he's perfectly good. They believe that he created humans in his own image and that he wants to have a good relationship with them. However, humans don't always accept God and so he tries to get us to come back to him. That's why he sent Jesus. Sometimes even Christians have difficult questions about life and wonder how God can let certain things happen. But they trust that he knows what he's doing – even if it doesn't always look that way to us. Christians believe that God can be a part of their everyday lives. What do you think?

Active Learning

1. Write up some questions that you would ask God if you could. Display these in class and try to group them into categories. Choose a couple of the questions and think about the responses that God might give. If you can invite a Christian into school to answer them for you, then even better.

2. Some Christians say that belief in God is an act of faith – you believe in it without evidence. But other Christians say that there is evidence that God exists. Find out about this 'evidence' – is it reliable? Does it prove that God exists? (You will need to look up reference books and the Internet, and this won't be easy!)
   - Evidence in arguments: the ontological argument; the first cause argument.
   - Indirect evidence: the argument from design; the existence of the natural world.
   - Direct evidence: miracles; the life of Jesus; religious experience.

3. Do people believe in God more or less in today's world than they did in the past? Find surveys in recent history where people were asked about their religious beliefs – compare these over time. You could also carry out your own research in your school – do people believe in God or not? Why?

4. How have people illustrated God in art throughout history? Have a look on Google Images and find different examples of how God has been depicted. You could also look into why Muslims and Jewish people are forbidden to make any artwork of God. Do you think God should be depicted or not? If you do, what are the best ways he is depicted and what are the worst?

5. Design your own page for a website called AskGod.com.

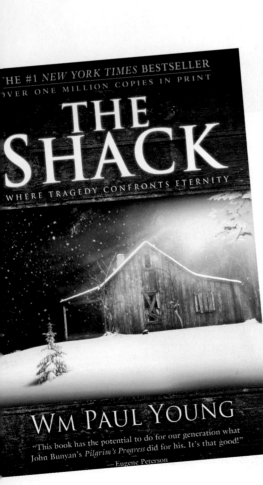

THE #1 NEW YORK TIMES BESTSELLER
OVER ONE MILLION COPIES IN PRINT

THE SHACK

WHERE TRAGEDY CONFRONTS ETERNITY

WM PAUL YOUNG

"This book has the potential to do for our generation what John Bunyan's *Pilgrim's Progress* did for his. It's that good!"
— Eugene Peterson

1. Have a class debate about the existence of God or invite people in to debate this for you and prepare questions for them.

2. What do you think is the strongest argument in favour of the existence of God? What is the strongest argument against it? Explore your thoughts on this.

3. Humanists recently displayed adverts on buses to encourage people to question their belief in God. Design an advert to go on a bus that a Christian might use to get people to believe in God.

4. Where do your own beliefs (or lack of beliefs) about God come from? Your parents? Friends? Society? Your own thinking? How have your beliefs about God changed throughout your life (if they have)?

On your own

1. Type 'God' into a search engine. What kind of sites come up? How many are religious? How many are arguing for or against the existence of God? How many are funny/serious? Prepare a short report about what you find.

2. Take the word 'God' and create your own acrostic explaining what people believe.

3. Christians believe that the stories in the Bible tell them what God is like. Choose one Bible story and explain what it tells us about the kind of being God is.

On a cold November day, Senga and Abi are sitting down by the harbour watching the boats come in and go out to the North Sea to catch fish.

Senga: Aye girl. I'll bet thay tuary-breeks is prayin that this weather'll brakk up a bit. Gaun be a caul yin oot there on the watter the nicht, an a richt frichtsome nicht the nicht an aw.

Abi: Aye, tis that richt enough. But prayin'll dae them nae guid.

Senga: Ach yer an aul haithin ye are. A prayer'll dae them nae hairm.

Abi: Mebbe no, but thay'll find that aw the time spent dae'in it wis wastit, fur ther'll nae be ony answer.

Senga: Nou, jist how dae ye ken that?

Abi: Leuk, fowk pray aw the time. Thay pray whan they're seek, thay pray whan thay're afeart, thay pray whan thay think thay're gan tae dee. Thay pray for fortuin an glore. An they niver get ony answer.

Senga: A few fowks maun.

Abi: Aye, mibbe ane or twa ilka sae lang.

Senga: Nou, the awmichtie canna dae awthing can he?

Abi: Hou no? He's the awmichtie efter aw. He makkit the hail warld an awthing in it did he no?

Senga: Aye, but that disna mean he's gan tae say 'aye' tae awthing.

Abi: Well he shoud. Whit ense dis he hae tae dae aw day?

Senga: He has a hail warld tae leuk efter.

Abi: Aye, weel-a-wat. So mebbe he coud stairt wi luekin efter thay puir taury-breeks.

Senga: It's thair chyce tae be ooot on the watter. The awmichtie dinna mak thaim.

Abi: Well mebbe the awmichtie shoud hae makkit fishin mair eith.

Senga: Aye, mebbe.

Translation: Senga wonders if the fishermen going out on the boats should offer up a little prayer to God for their protection out at sea, seeing as it's a horrid night. Abi argues that this would be pointless. She claims that people pray for all sorts of things and none of them ever seem to happen. Senga replies that God can't be doing everything all the time, which Abi thinks is a weak argument. Abi thinks that if God is all-powerful and wants the best for everyone, he should be prepared to answer everyone's prayers. Senga replies that God might not want to answer every prayer, but Abi thinks that if God wants to look after the beings he created, he should either do so or make life easier in the first place. Why should the fisherman have to face such dangers doing their work? Couldn't God have made it easier for them?

Prayer

Christians believe that prayer is talking with God. It is a way of expressing their hopes and their fears, and asking God to guide them in life or help them, or do the same for others. You can even ask Christians to pray for you or someone you know – maybe someone who is ill. Christians believe that God listens to your prayers and answers them, but not always in the way you expected. Some Christians believe that he answers only the prayers of those who truly believe in him; others believe that he answers prayers only when the prayer is asking for something good. Sometimes, when prayers do not seem to be answered, this can be quite confusing – even for Christians. This is why prayer is also an act of faith. What do you think?

⚙ *Active Learning*

1. Draw up a list of things that it would be ok for a Christian to pray for and things it would not be ok to pray for.

2. Create a visual display exploring things in the world that could be prayed for. Perhaps you could write the prayers that might be said about these things underneath images of them.

3. Find out people's views on prayer. Do people pray these days? How do they do it? What for? What happens if they don't get what they prayed for?

4. Many Christians believe in miracles. These are supernatural events caused by God – sometimes in response to prayer. Find out about one miracle that Christians believe God has performed. Describe what happened and express your own view about it. What other explanations could there be for this event?

5. Christians have prayers that they say together. Find out the words to one of the following prayers. What does this prayer express? When is it said? Why is it used? Design a fact sheet or a multi-media presentation about this.
   a. the Lord's Prayer (the 'Our Father')
   b. Hail Mary
   c. the Benediction
   d. the Lord's my Shepherd
   e. the Desiderata
   f. the Selkirk Grace.

💬 *Talking and listening*

- What is prayer? Have you ever prayed? What did you pray for? What happened after your prayer?
- Do you know anyone who has prayed for something and their prayer seems to have been answered?
- Is it ok to pray for some things and not others?
- What do Christians think the point of prayer is?
- Do you think praying 'works'?

1. Here are some statements. Choose one you agree with and one you disagree with; explain your views on each.
   a. 'If praying helps you cope where's the harm in that?'
   b. 'When others know you're praying for them it helps them – nothing wrong with that.'
   c. 'People pray for things all the time, but disasters still happen and so do wars and disease.'
   d. 'There's no point in praying because no one's listening.'
   e. 'Some prayers are answered and some are not – God knows best after all.'
   f. 'If God knows everything, why does anyone need to pray in the first place?'

2. Choose one of the formal prayers you looked at in Active Learning task 5. Rewrite this prayer, expressing its meaning in another form. You could do rap, poetry or song, or write it in your own local dialect.

3. Christian prayers are sometimes expressed in the form of hymns and songs. Find one Christian song that expresses prayer-like ideas. Write your own explanation of what the song is expressing.

4. Some Christians think that praying together is better than praying on your own. Some think that praying in a church is better than praying at home. Express your views on this and discuss with someone else in your class.

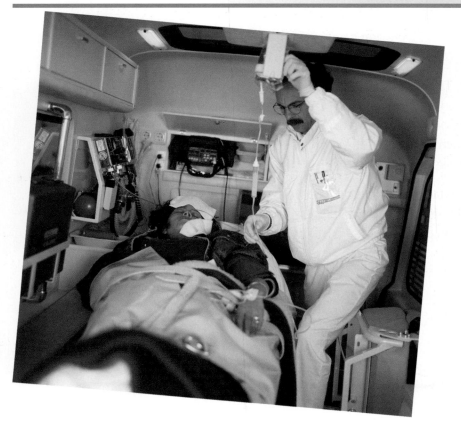

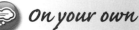 **On your own**

1. How has prayer changed through history? Find an example of a Christian prayer from as many different centuries as possible. How have the ideas and the words changed? What different things have people prayed for throughout the ages? You could display your findings along a timeline of history.

2. Some prayers are linked to special events or times in Christian life. Find an example of a prayer linked to a couple of the following:
   a. infant baptism
   b. marriage
   c. funerals
   d. Easter
   e. Christmas
   f. Remembrance Day
   g. mealtimes.

3. Sometimes a prayer can just be concentrating on an image rather than saying words. This makes it more like meditation. Find a good image for a Christian to meditate on.

Connor and Jack are both 12. They live next door to each other and they're best friends.

Connor: I like computer games and football. I like pizza.
Jack: I like computer games and football. I also like pizza.
Connor: I go to church with my parents on a Sunday.
Jack: I go to church with my parents on a Sunday.

Connor: At church we say prayers and sing hymns.
Jack: At church we say prayers and sing hymns.
Connor: At Christmas, I celebrate the birthday of Jesus. I like the presents too.
Jack: At Christmas, I celebrate the birthday of Jesus. I also like presents.
Connor: I believe that God made the Universe and everything in it.
Jack: So do I.
Connor: I am taught that Jesus died for our sins.
Jack: Me too.
Connor: I believe that Jesus taught us what was right and wrong by leaving behind his teachings and the example of his life.

Jack: I believe that Jesus taught us what was right and wrong too. I follow his teachings and example as well.
Connor: I believe that you should help other people whenever you can.
Jack: I believe you should help other people whenever you can.
Connor: I think that when you die you might go to Heaven.
Jack: I think that when you die you might go to Heaven.
Connor: I believe that we can have a happy life if we live our lives like Jesus did.
Jack: I believe we can have a happy life if we live our lives like Jesus did.
Connor: I am a Christian.
Jack: I am a Christian.
Connor: I am a Protestant.
Jack: I am a Catholic.

Talking and listening

- What is a Catholic?
- What is a Protestant?
- In what ways are Catholics and Protestants the same/ different?
- In some parts of Scotland, Catholics and Protestants go to different schools. What do you think about this?
- Catholic schools and non-denominational schools have different RME. Why do you think this is?

Catholics and Protestants

Imagine two people read the same book – what do you think the chances are that they'd think exactly the same thing about it? The Christian faith has many groups, sects and denominations. One major division is between Roman Catholics and Protestants.

Until the sixteenth century, in Western Europe there was really only one type of Christian church. The head of this was the Pope, who lived in Rome. Then, Martin Luther protested against what he saw as the faults of the church. From that point on, it split into two denominations, Protestant and Roman Catholic. This division, called

Pope Benedict XVI

the Reformation, became an important part of the history of Scotland. In some parts of the country, it is still a big issue. There are separate schools that Roman Catholic parents send their children to, although in these schools the only subject that is taught differently is RME. In other parts of Scotland, nobody pays much attention to all this, and Catholic and Protestant children go to the same school. Roman Catholic Christians and Protestant Christians have the same basic beliefs about most things to do with their faith. Unfortunately, it's sometimes the differences that make the news. Why is that?

Active Learning

1. Find out about the protest of Martin Luther in sixteenth-century Germany that led to the split within the Christian Church. Create a report about his ninety-five theses (points of disagreement with the Church), explaining how they led to the division. How did the Church respond to Luther's protests?

2. John Knox brought the Reformation to Scotland. Write a fact file (or interactive display) about him. Who was he? What did he do? What changes did he bring to Christianity in Scotland? How did the Church respond to him? You could also look at the effect of Irish migration on the Catholic–Protestant divide in the west of Scotland.

3. In some parts of Scotland there are separate schools for children of Roman Catholic parents. What are the arguments for and against this? You could look at the Scottish Catholic Education Service (**www.sces.uk.com**) for some ideas. Perhaps you could invite someone in to discuss this – or link up with a Roman Catholic school if you're not in one yourself. You could also look at the guidelines for RME for Roman Catholic schools, which are different to those for non-denominational schools. You'll find these at **www. ltscotland.org.uk/curriculumforexcellence/rme/rerc/index.asp**.

4. The Roman Catholic Church in Scotland remains one organisation. However, the Protestant Church has split further into many different groups. Make a list of these different groups. For each group you name, write one major belief that is linked to it.

5. If you can, visit one Protestant church and one Roman Catholic church. What are the similarities and differences between the two? Watch an act of worship, if you can. How are things done differently and what things are the same? If you can't do this, many churches now offer virtual tours online. There's also a virtual church at **http:// churchoffools.com/enter-church/index.html**, where you can become a character and actually take part in a service.

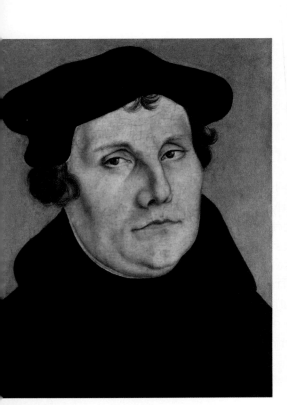

Martin Luther

1. Have a debate in class based on one of the following statements:
    a. 'Having separate schools for Roman Catholic and Protestant children divides Scottish Society and is not a good thing.'
    b. 'Children do not know there is any 'difference' between Catholics and Protestants until their parents say there is.'
    c. 'There's nothing wrong with keeping your identity by sending your child to a Catholic school.'

2. What differences in beliefs and practices are there between Catholics and Protestants? Make a list and decide whether you think they are major or minor ones. What similarities are there?

3. What things could be done in Scotland to bring Catholic and Protestant communities closer together? Plan a campaign that would do this – you could design posters and leaflets.

On your own

1. Catholic–Protestant tension in Scotland is usually called sectarianism. The Scottish Government wants to tackle this problem. Have a look at **www.ltscotland.org.uk/antisectarian**. How can sectarianism be ended? Look at the charity Nil by Mouth, which also tackles sectarianism (**http://nilbymouth.org**).

2. How did Christianity arrive in Scotland in the first place? Find out about the lives of Saints Ninian (**www.whithorn.com/saint-ninian.htm**), Kentigern (**www.newadvent.org/cathen/08620a. htm**) and Columba (**www.rampantscotland.com/famous/ blfamcolumba.htm**). What did they do to bring the faith to this country? How did it change Scotland?

3. If you have looked at the Roman Catholic RME guidelines, you should also look at the non-denominational ones at **www.ltscotland.org.uk/curriculumforexcellence/rme/ nondenominational/index.asp**. In what ways are the two different? What are your views about this?

Talking and listening

- These are stained glass windows. Why do you think they are in a church?
- Which of them do you like best? Why?
- Religious art is there to help religious people. How might it do this?
- Stained glass and other artworks in a church can be very expensive. Do you think churches should be spending money on them?
- Why do you think many Christians like to express their faith through art?

Christian art

You will find stained glass windows in churches all around Scotland. They originally had two purposes. The first was to tell a Bible story in pictures at a time when many people could not read. The other was to create a colourful, restful atmosphere inside a church. Nowadays they might also remember a famous person or event. Even the most sparsely decorated Protestant churches may still have elaborate stained glass windows. They might also have wall paintings, tapestries and so on. In Roman Catholic churches you will also see statues of religious figures and often artwork depicting the last days of Jesus – known as the Stations of the Cross.

In Orthodox churches, the artwork can be even more extravagant. Here, metal lanterns may hang from the ceilings, icons (holy paintings) will be present and even the Bible in the church might be richly decorated with precious jewels. Why? As well as helping Christians concentrate during worship and teaching them about their faith, carefully made artwork lets people know that faith matters. It also expresses many Christian beliefs – without ever saying a word. Would churches be the same without it all?

Active Learning

1. Choose a Bible story, a figure from Christianity or a Christian belief you have explored during this section. Create your own stained glass window to depict this. You could go to the Art department and use glass or go to CDT and use plastics, or just stay in RME and use acetate or coloured paper.

2. Many of the world's great pieces of art have Christian themes. Choose one and display a copy of it in your class. Include information about who made it and why, and what Christian beliefs it expresses. You could create an exhibition in your school.

3. In the Orthodox churches, icons are not just works of art; they are regarded as holy objects. Find out about how they are made, where they are placed and how people treat them. Create a report of your findings.

4. Jesus and Mary are the two figures in Christianity who are depicted in art most often. Find examples of artwork depicting them as either Madonna and Child or the Pieta (after the death of Jesus). How does the artist convey his or her idea of these two figures?

5. Imagine that a local Christian church has commissioned you to create a new piece of religious art for their building. It has to be linked to Christianity (obviously) and to be as modern as possible. You can use any medium to produce it. Set out your designs for this artwork and, if you have the time, make it.

1. Here are two opposite viewpoints. Discuss in class and note down the range of opinions expressed about them.
   a. 'Great works of art are a good way to show how much your faith means to you. It does not matter how much they cost.'
   b. 'Christians should not be spending great sums of money on artwork – they should be using the money to help people instead.'

2. Choose one of the following events. What kind of Christian artwork would be suitable to put on a card at this time?
   a. Christmas
   b. Easter
   c. the birth of a new child
   d. wedding
   e. death of a close relative.

3. Is modern religious art better than the classic art of the past? Explain your own views on this.

4. Graffiti is thought by some to be a modern form of art that gets people talking. Should Christians paint Christian graffiti in public places? What would it look like? Get some views from people in your class about this (you could design some too… in your jotters though!).

💬 *On your own*

1. Visit an art gallery if there's one locally. How much of the art there is religious art? How much of it is Christian? You could make your own guide to the Christian art in the gallery. (If you can't get to an art gallery, then visit the website of the National Galleries of Scotland at **www.nationalgalleries.org** or the National Gallery in London at **www.nationalgallery.org.uk**).

2. Even if you're not near an art gallery, you probably live close to some kind of memorial monument like a Remembrance Day cenotaph or even a graveyard. How does the artwork here express Christian beliefs? You could look back at some of your work in chapter 21 for ideas here.

3. Some artists have expressed Christian ideas in modern art in controversial ways. One is a project to tell the Bible story completely in Lego – see **www.thebricktestament.com**. Do you think this is a good way to help people understand the Bible?

The beginning
of things

In ancient Mesopotamia… In the Enuma Elish the tale is told of the mighty beings known as Apsu and Tiamat – one male and one female. Their children are gods and monsters, and there is chaos everywhere. Tiamat tries to get things under control, but Marduk, of whom Tiamat is an ancestor, is chosen to take the lead against her. Tiamat is helped by Kingu, but a mighty battle with Marduk follows. Marduk kills Tiamat and cuts her body into two. From one half he makes the heavens and the other the Earth, and he uses the blood of Kingu to create human beings.

In ancient Egypt… There was but water (Nu) – chaotic and seething. Then came Ra, the mighty Sun God. He produced four great children: Shu and Tefnut the air and clouds, Geb the Earth and Nut the sky. Humans came from the tears of Ra, but they were wicked and he vowed to destroy them. When almost all were dead, he spared the last ones and the human race began again.

In ancient China… An ancient giant egg was filled with the being Pan Ku. He cracked the egg from within; some parts of the shell fell to become Earth and some floated upwards to become the heavens. When Pan Ku died, parts of his body became the stars and Moon and his breath became the air. But there was chaos, and out of this chaos came two great lights – mighty forces that remain to this day. Yin and yang; male and female; darkness and light; Earth and sky.

In the lands of the Aztecs… There was nothing but darkness. The God Omecihuatl, who was both male and female in one being, watched over this darkness, brooding and alone. Then Omecihuatl gave birth to four great gods who set about creating all things on Earth.

These four represent north, south, east and west. The God of the west, Tezcatlipoca, was sacrificed to create the Sun and give life to all. But arguments among the gods led to war, and many died. One god after another became the Sun.

In the islands of the Pacific… There was nothing but ocean and the world of the spirits. There was a rock between them on which lived Biki and Kele, Atungaki and Maimoa'o Longona and others too. Their children took the sky and the underworld. One day the mighty Maui gave an old man a fishing rod. With this, the old man pulled from the depths of the ocean many of the islands of the Pacific… or perhaps it was the great God Tangaroa, who created everything from nothing.

In the frozen north of the Inuit… Two giants had a daughter who they named Sedna. But she ate all the food so they took her out to sea in a canoe and tried to throw her into the ocean. She clung to the canoe but they chopped off her fingers. She sank to the sea floor and her body became the living things in the water. Her spiritual presence is still there, and without her the sea would not give up its life-giving nourishment.

Creation myths

Stories about how the Universe began usually involve mighty gods, giants, monsters, battles and wars. Some people take them quite literally and believe that they really happened, but others say they shouldn't be taken too seriously. Some people take a view that while the stories are not factually true, they tell us something about how life began. They are full of metaphors and symbolism (where things stand for other things). All around the world, these creation stories have many similarities: chaos and disorganisation is replaced by order and calm, usually through the actions of a god or group of gods. Sometimes the origin of these gods is explained; sometimes it's not. Creation stories are like other kinds of story, in that they help the listener to make sense of something. Do you think these stories help people to understand something difficult? Do they help you?

Active Learning

1. Choose one of the creation myths and retell it in the form of a story board or another visual display. Think about the music and sound effects that might go with the story.

2. On a world map, mark the countries where there are creation stories. Design a simple illustration to mark each location.

3. Most of the creation myths focus heavily on the natural world and natural forces, because these have always been important to humans' survival. Think about the elements of nature below. Find out how each one helps us to survive and how different groups around the world have treated it with special reverence.
   a. Earth
   b. Moon
   c. Sun
   d. trees
   e. wind
   f. rain.

4. There is no Scottish creation myth (as such). Write one!

Talking and listening

- What do some of these stories have in common? What differences are there?
- Do you think they are a helpful way to explain how the Universe began?
- Why are there so many different creation stories around the world?
- How do you think the Universe began?

1. Discuss this statement in class: 'Creation myths are just fairy stories that we should abandon now that we live in a scientific age.'

2. Do you think it is important to respect other people's beliefs about how the Universe began? Would it be right to challenge these creation stories? Explain your views.

3. Find out more about one of the creation myths you have looked at in this section. Now rewrite the myth as either a poem or an illustrated magazine article.

On your own

1. Find one more example of a creation myth and write the story in your own words.

2. Ask as many people as you can the question: 'How do you think the Universe began?' Report your findings using a graph.

3. The writer Terry Pratchett has created a whole Universe of his own called Discworld, which exists on a turtle's back. Find out about Pratchett's Discworld by visiting www.terrypratchett.co.uk. Is his view of the Universe any different from (or similar to) any of the creation myths you have explored?

How the rivers got here

Long ago there was nothing except Guthi-guthi, the great spirit who lived in the sky. Guthi-guthi decided to create the land and everything on it. He decided that the land needed water because it was dry and bare and nothing was growing, so he called for a water snake called Weowie. But Weowie was trapped inside a mountain and couldn't hear him. Guthi-guthi got angry and struck the mountain, which split in two. Weowie came gushing out, and where he slithered he left behind rivers and water-holes. Now the land wasn't dry any more.

Based on a story told by Aunty Beryl Carmichael of the Ngiyaampaa people of New South Wales at http://australianmuseum.net.au/movie/Creation-Story.

How the water got to the plains

A long time ago the land was dry. All the wells were filled with dust… except one. At night, two greedy men called Weeri and Walawidbit went to the well and took what was left of the water. When the people woke up they realised that there was no water left and the two men were missing. A hunting party was sent out and soon caught up with the men. A spearman took aim and threw his spear. It burst the water carrier but the two thieves didn't notice and kept on running, spilling the water all over the plains. Where the spear landed, water holes sprang up.

Based on a story told by Olga Miller of the Butchulla people of Fraser Island at www.australianmuseum.net.au/movie/How-the-water-got-to-the-plains.

Why the crocodile rolls

On the coast there was a little girl, Min-na-wee, who was grumpy, bad-tempered and liked to cause trouble. When she got older and was not chosen to have a husband, her troublemaking got even worse. Eventually the people decided to punish her by rolling her over and over again in the dirt. She ran to the sea to wash off the muck and here she asked the evil spirits to turn her into a nasty animal so she could have her revenge. They turned her into a crocodile. One day one of the people who'd punished her came to the water; she grabbed him and rolled him around and around just like they had punished her. And that's why crocodiles roll when killing their prey.

Based on a story told by Jiller Rii of the Gwini people of Kulumburru at www.australianmuseum.net.au/movie/Min-na-wee-Why-the-crocodile-rolls.

- All over Australia, Aboriginal people have stories like this. What do you think these stories are for?
- Which story do you like best and why?
- Has anyone ever told you a story about how something came to be the way it is today?
- Do you think stories like this help people to understand life?
- Does it matter if these stories actually happened or not?

The Dreamtime

The Aboriginal peoples of Australia are formed by many different tribal groups across this vast country. These groups all believe that great beings, called the Dreamtime ancestors, moved across the Earth creating mountains, rocks, rivers and water holes. You might be surprised to know that we have similar stories in Scotland: Ailsa Craig in the Firth of Clyde is said to be a great boulder hurled into the sea by an angry giant. The belief that the land and its inhabitants are gifts from spiritual ancestors helps the Aboriginal peoples to care for their surroundings. The Dreamtime stories also explain the origins of things. What do you think of this?

 *Active Learning*

1. Each of the three stories on page 117 is available as a video on the website of the Australian Museum. In class, retell one of the stories in whatever format you like. The stories are mostly passed down by Aboriginal people through storytelling – perhaps you could retell the story in this simple way!

2. Many more examples of Dreamtime stories are available online. Search for some and retell them in your own way.

3. Aboriginal people have a very distinctive style of art. Here is an example. Create an aboriginal artwork based on one of the Dreamtime stories.

4. Look at your own country or the place where you live. Choose a local natural feature and make up your own 'Scottish Dreamtime story' about how it came to be.

5. Because of the Dreamtime stories, the Aboriginal peoples feel very attached to the land. This sometimes leads to conflicts with the Australian government about the treatment of ancestral lands. Visit the following websites and make your own report about the different views on Aboriginal rights:
   - http://aboriginalrightscoalition.wordpress.com/
   - http://home.vicnet.net.au/~aar/
   - http://indigenousrights.net.au/organisations.asp
   - www.australia.gov.au

1. Get everyone in the class to pick out three bits from the stories you have looked at in this section and write them on cards. Now put the heading of each story on another card and try to place the cards under the correct heading.

2. Many Australians believe that it is important to respect Aboriginal beliefs, but others think that beliefs about the land should not get in the way of 'progress' – using the resources that the land has to offer. Discuss this in class.

3. Go through the Dreamtime stories you have looked at in this section. Now compare the features of these stories with the other creation stories you explored in the previous section. What similarities and differences are there?

4. Complete the following sentences in relation to the creation stories and Dreamtime stories you have looked at so far:
   a. 'One thing I find strange about these stories is…'
   b. 'One thing I like about these stories is…'
   c. 'One thing I don't like about these stories is…'
   d. 'I think these stories might be helpful for listeners because…'
   e. 'I think these stories are…'

On your own

1. Uluru/Ayers Rock is a famous Australian landmark. It is both a major tourist attraction and a site of great spiritual meaning for local Aboriginal peoples. Find out about Uluru/Ayers Rock and write a short report about it, explaining what it is, the beliefs surrounding it and the tension between tourism and respecting a sacred site. (See **www.environment.gov.au/parks/uluru/index.html**.)

2. There are many different Aboriginal groups in modern Australia. Find out how many there are and what they are called. On a map of Australia, mark the locations of each group.

3. The Dreamtime is remembered in the Songlines. These are tracks across the land that remember Dreamtime events in music, dance and story. Listen to some Aboriginal music: go to **www.youtube. com/watch?v=dFGvNxBqYFI** or find out about Geoffrey Gurrumul Yunupingu, a modern Aboriginal singer who has had worldwide success (**www.gurrumul.com**). What instruments are used? What kind of sound is made? How might this music help Aboriginal peoples in their spiritual life?

Imagine God kept a diary…

Day '0'
You know, I really must do something about all this nothingness. I keep meaning to create something but I can never find the time. Right, I'll start tomorrow.

Day 1
Ok, sorted out day and night today – that makes the whole time thing a bit more meaningful.

Day 2
Fixed the firmament today, which means that there can be a difference between the land and the sky.

Day 3
Thought the land was looking a bit bare, so I made some seas to separate it out a bit. Spruced the land up a bit by adding some trees and plants.

Day 4
Had a good idea about the lighting – going to call them the Sun and the Moon. Also added some stars, which will look like tiny twinkling lights.

Day 5
Made some birds to twitter about the sky today. Also, I thought the waters were looking a bit empty so I filled them with creatures of all sorts.

Day 6
Right, that's more or less it. I've added a whole lot of colourful life forms everywhere. Did the humans as well – they were the trickiest bit of the whole thing, especially the souls. I decided to make them a bit like myself. Was going to do just a man, but thought maybe a woman would be a good idea too.

Day 7
Decided to put my feet up today and have a rest. I think I've done a pretty good job even if I say so myself. Had quite an interesting chat with Adam yesterday, Eve was off checking out the trees. Hope they follow my advice…

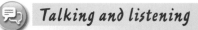
Talking and listening

- What do you know about the Bible's creation story?
- In what ways is it similar to or different from any of the other creation stories you have explored?
- Do you believe that the Bible's creation story is true or not? Why do you believe one thing or the other?
- Do you think all Christians believe that the Bible's creation story is actually true?
- If the creation story is true (in any way), why do you think God made things when he didn't have to?

The Bible's creation story

This version of creation is shared by Christians, Jews and Muslims. Over six days, God makes everything there is, finishing off with humans. Some Christians think this story happened exactly the way the Bible says it; others think that it is not factually true but is full of symbols and meaning. Finally, some Christians think this story is just a myth to help people understand something very complicated. So some Christians believe that there was a real Adam and Eve who were the first humans; others say that this is just a story explaining the relationship between God and humans. What do you think?

 Active Learning

1. Retell the Bible's six-day creation story in cartoon form. You could do this in the old-fashioned strip cartoon way or make an animation. Alternatively, you could tell the story in the form of a song or a poem, or even do it as a puppet show.

2. According to Christians, the six-day creation story is followed by the story of Adam and Eve and how their relationship with God went wrong because of their disobedience. Find out the details of this story and retell it in your own way. What is the message here?

3. Think about the kind of music that should accompany each day of the creation story. This could be classical or modern (or a mixture of both). You could create a PowerPoint presentation about the six days of creation, with one image and one piece of music for each day.

4. Many great works of art explore the Christian creation story. Find some examples and display each one. Get people in your class to say what they think of each one as a way of depicting parts of the creation story.

5. Christians who understand the Bible's creation story as being factually true have to face some difficulties. Invite someone into school to answer these questions, or look at some websites to see if you can get answers to them. Search for terms such as 'Biblical literalism', 'Creation Science' and 'Creationism'.
   a. Where did Adam and Eve's son find a wife?
   b. Why have so many species throughout Earth's history become extinct? Did God change his mind?
   c. What about the scientific evidence that living things have changed over time instead of being created originally as they are now?
   d. Was it fair of God to give Adam and Eve a free choice and then punish them for their choice?
   e. If God knows everything, then wouldn't he have known that Adam and Eve would disobey him?

1. Here are some statements about the Christian creation story. For each one, think about arguments supporting or opposing it.
   a. 'There's no reason to think that the Christian creation story is any more true than the others that exist around the world.'
   b. 'If the Bible says it, we should believe it.'
   c. 'Christians who believe the Bible's creation story are just being childish.'
   d. 'Christians who believe the Bible's creation story are showing faith.'
   e. 'Science has shown that the Bible's creation story is untrue.'

2. Using the story of Adam and Eve, and their decision to turn away from God, write a series of diary entries. You could split the class into three: one section doing God's diary, one Adam's and one Eve's.

3. Some Christians say that the Bible's creation story is just a simple way to explain something that we couldn't possibly understand because the maths and science involved would be too complicated. What do you think of this view?

On your own

1. Creationism is the belief that the Bible story is factually true. Creation Science tries to use science to back up the creation story. Visit one Creationist and one Creation Science website (for example, www.creationism.org and www.csm.org.uk/index. php). How well do you think they explain their beliefs? What questions would you like to ask them? You could also look at the websites of those opposed to creationism and creation science (such as http://richarddawkins.net and www.secularism.org.uk/ darwinsbirthdaychallengetocreati.html).

2. Some people think that the Bible's creation story should be taught alongside scientific views in Science classes. In the USA, this is a big issue that has ended up in the courts. What do you think? Should religious views be taught alongside Science? Carry out a survey of people's views about this and report your findings to the class.

3. Do you think it makes any difference what you believe about how the Universe began? Does it affect your daily life in any way? Write your own thoughts about this and discuss your views with others.

Findlay-John MacHaggerty has been marking exams for many years. His speciality is religion and science. When pupils are asked about religious and scientific views of the beginning of the Universe, they sometimes get a bit confused. So Findlay-John has decided to put them right about it…

Dear SQA RMPS Candidate,

I hope you're enjoying your studies. It's time for me to get a few things straight in your confused little brainboxes so that you can answer that Big Bang question and get full marks. First of all, let me explain what the big bang is *not*. It is not when two planets crashed into each other – there were no planets to do any crashing. It is not when a planet exploded – there wasn't anything there in the first place. Finally, it was not the work of a race of super-intelligent and unbelievably powerful alien beings (as far as I know). So, dear student, let me try to put it all as simply as I can.

First of all, at the moment of the Big Bang all matter in the Universe was created. There was absolutely nothing before it. Every single physical thing that exists today was created at the Big Bang. Secondly, space itself was created at the Big Bang. So things didn't explode into space, space itself expanded. Thirdly, there was no 'before the Big Bang' because the Big Bang was the beginning of time too. I know, you think time is an idea instead of a real thing, but it's not – it's a physical property.

So dearest candidate, no one said the Big Bang was going to be easy, but then who said school would be easy? Sometimes the things worth learning are the ones that make your brain hurt a bit…

Talking and listening

- Who has heard of the Big Bang in your class? How much do they know about it?
- Did anything Findlay-John wrote surprise you?
- What do you think of the idea of time itself beginning? What about the idea of time as a 'thing'?
- If the Big Bang is correct, what might that do to belief in God?
- How do you feel about the fact that everything that makes you must have been around at the time of the Big Bang?

The Big Bang

Yes, in one way it's very complicated but in another way it's very simple. The Big Bang is a scientific theory that says that at some point space, matter and time came into being. Scientists are not sure why this happened, but they claim that there is evidence of it happening. First of all, the whole Universe is expanding. If we run that expanding in reverse we get to a starting point – the Big Bang. Secondly, the Universe is still hot. This heat is probably left over from the Big Bang (think about how long it takes your oven to cool down after you switch it off). Thirdly, everything that's in the Universe is there in just the amounts that you would get if it had all started in a Big Bang. It's as if the recipe for the Universe had to start with a Big Bang. Now, what caused the Big Bang? Scientifically no one knows, but some people think that it means creation by a God is not needed – the Universe just created itself. Other people think that the Big Bang was maybe the way God made things. No one's sure of course, because there's no evidence either way – it's just what you believe. What do you think?

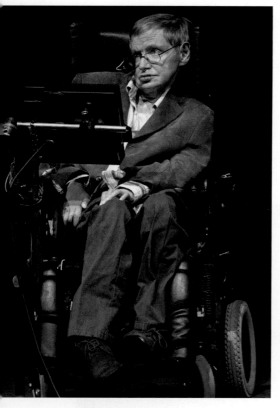

Stephen Hawking

Active Learning

1. When they're asked about how the Universe began, people often reply with something linked to the Big Bang theory. Sometimes they have a very good knowledge of this and sometimes they don't. Design a questionnaire that asks people about their views about how the Universe began. You could also ask them to explain what they think the Big Bang theory means for belief in a God or gods as creator(s). Present your findings in a short report with text, graphs and illustrations. You should make sure you do this questionnaire with any pupils in your school who are studying certificate RMPS.

2. Create a display on the Big Bang, including text about the science as well as artwork depicting space, matter and time.

3. Many great works of art have been made depicting the Christian creation story. Have any great artworks depicted the Big Bang? Search Google Images for 'Big Bang artwork' and see what you come up with. How well does the art depict the ideas behind the Big Bang? If you were going to depict the Big Bang, how would you do it?

4. Many famous scientists have tried or are trying to work out the details of the Big Bang. Design a fact file about one of the following, including information about their theories:
   a. Albert Einstein
   b. Georges Lemaitre
   c. Edwin Hubble
   d. Stephen Hawking.

Progress Check

1. Design an A–Z of the Big Bang. You can illustrate this if you like. (Your senior RMPS pupils may have done something similar. Compare yours with theirs – whose is the best?)

2. Turn what you have learned about the Big Bang into a song or a rhyme. You could put it to suitable music and sing it in class.

3. Here are some statements about the Big Bang and its link (or not) with religious belief. For each one, say whether you agree, disagree or are not sure and explain your choice.
   a. 'The Big Bang means there's no need for a God.'
   b. 'Perhaps God made everything using the Big Bang.'
   c. 'The Big Bang is just a theory – you can't prove it.'
   d. 'If God made the Big Bang, we'd have to ask who made God.'
   e. 'To say that the Universe 'just happened' makes no sense.'

4. Ask your teacher to show you some SQA exam questions on the Big Bang at Intermediate 1, 2 and Higher level (there are also some at Standard Grade level). Try some out and get your teacher to mark them. Questions (with answers!) can also be found on the SQA website at **www.sqa.org.uk/sqa/6957.html**.

On your own

1. Find out more about the evidence for the Big Bang. The following websites should help:
   b. **www.bbc.co.uk/science/space/origins/bigbang**
   c. **www.big-bang-theory.com**
   d. **www.historyforkids.org/scienceforkids/physics/space/bigbang.htm**
   e. **www.esa.int/esaKIDSen/SEMSZ5WJD1E_OurUniverse_0.html**

2. Some people believe that knowing how everything began is important in helping us understand who we are; others think that it doesn't really make any difference to our lives. What do you think? What are the views of your parents and friends?

3. The Big Bang theory is usually only studied in the senior years of school, but now you're doing so in the junior years. Could it be studied right at the start of primary school? Think about how you could teach what you have learned in this section to P1 pupils, and set out your ideas.

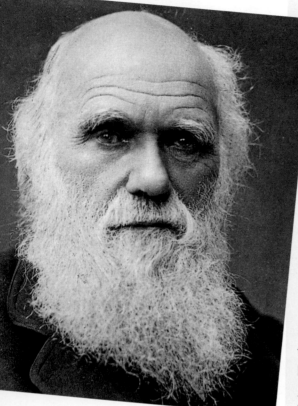

From 1831 to 1836, Charles Darwin travelled the world aboard a ship called The Beagle. *His discoveries on this voyage led to the publication of* The Origin of Species, *which challenged the very idea of creation by God. Darwin himself was troubled about what his theory meant for all the things that Christians believed. Here's what he might have written in his diary…*

I just don't get it. I am taught that God created all life at the beginning as it is now – so why all these fossils of life forms that are no longer here? Did God change his mind and kill things off? And the parts of the body we humans share with other animals – did God have only a few ideas that he copied and changed around a bit? Why do some living things seem to have body parts that they don't use – like wings on flightless penguins, as I saw in South America. I also saw creatures that I have seen nowhere else in the world – why would God create creatures especially for that land and not elsewhere? Can it be that what we are taught from childhood is wrong? Are we still to believe in a creation in six days merely a few thousand years ago, when all my studies of the rocks on this good Earth tell me that this planet has existed for many millions of years?

I am sorely troubled. It seems that with each new discovery I make, I am challenging the authority of the almighty God himself. What will my dear wife Emma, who is so strong in her religious faith, make of it all? What will the public think of me – will I be remembered for ever more as the wicked man who challenged God himself? Yesterday I looked at the grassy riverbank – all manner of life was there. Everywhere I looked, one insect was preying upon another; each leaf straining towards the sunlight, not caring if it blocked the light for others and so let them die. It seemed to be a violent struggle for life where only the strongest would survive. Is that the world of harmony, the 'all things bright and beautiful' that our Christian teachers speak of? Or is the world ruled by the blind uncaring hand of the forces of nature? Is it right for one simple man such as I to unleash this doubt and trouble upon the world? Would it be better to keep silent?

Talking and listening

- What do you know about Darwin and his theory of evolution?
- Do you think nature is peaceful and harmonious or a violent struggle?
- What things do humans share with other animals?
- From what you know about Christian beliefs about creation, why is Darwin's theory a challenge?
- Do you think someone could believe in both the Christian creation story and evolution?

Darwinian evolution

Darwin's theory is really quite simple. Living things have to be able to fit into their environment. If they don't, they die. They fit in because over many millions of years they adapt to their surroundings and pass this benefit on to their offspring. If their surroundings change they have to adapt again, and if they don't they become extinct. Darwin called this evolution by natural selection. It means that nature 'selects' the most suitable living things to survive in a particular environment.

Let's say that tomorrow the whole world becomes a few degrees colder. The animals most likely to survive are the ones already adapted to the cold, like polar bears. Animals that need warmer temperatures to live might not make it. Darwin didn't know how this worked, but the answer came long after his death with the discovery of DNA. Every new living thing has slightly different DNA from its parents, which might help it adapt… or not. Darwin's theory stirred things up because it challenged the Christian creation story: people still argue about it long after his death.

Active Learning

1. Find out about Darwin's voyage on *The Beagle*. Where did he go? What did he find? How did he come up with his theory of evolution? You could split up as a class and look at different parts of the voyage. You could plot it on a world map and show what he did where; you could make this a multi-media experience using clips from YouTube.

2. Darwin used evidence from many different subjects in his theory. Ask some teachers to tell you a bit about how their own subject played its part in uncovering evolutionary theory.
   a. Biology: similarities between species, speciation, adaptation, vestigial organs, breeding processes, embryology
   b. Physics: dating the age of the Earth
   c. Chemistry: DNA
   d. Geography: fossils and geology, age of the Earth, geographical variations in life forms, populations, migrations, changes to land masses on Earth (such as plate tectonics)
   e. History: the history of the creation/evolution debate
   f. Home Economics: the relationship between nutrition and health, food supplies and population.

→

3. Find out how scientists think the species below became extinct or had to adapt to change. What was it that the animals couldn't adapt to? You could also consider animals that are currently in danger of becoming extinct. What is threatening their existence? The website **www.ypte.org.uk/environmental/extinction/27** will help.
   a. the dinosaurs
   b. the dodo
   c. the peppered moth.

4. Carry out your own research into evolution just by looking around your garden (or your school grounds). The banded snail is being used by scientists to measure evolutionary change and you can get involved too. Go to **www.evolutionmegalab.org** to sign up and start contributing to real scientific research.

5. Create a display in your classroom showing the unpleasant side to nature. You could entitle your display 'The Struggle for Survival'. Try to include as many different life forms as you can (including humans).

 **Progress Check**

1. Have a debate in class using this statement: 'You can't believe in evolution and creation by God at the same time – you have to believe in one or the other'. Again, if you can get adults to come in and debate this for you then it might be even better. Think about the questions you might like to ask them.

2. Imagine you could write a letter to Darwin. What would you tell him about what happened to his theory after his death?

3. Here is another statement to discuss in class: 'Evolution means that humans are just another animal. Is that a good thing or a bad thing?'

On your own

1. Darwin's home, Downe House in Kent, is now a museum dedicated to his life and work. Visit its website (**www.english-heritage.org.uk/server.php?show=nav.14922**). You can even take a virtual tour of his study and find out about the experiments he did there.

2. Many others helped Darwin develop his theory through their own scientific research. Find out about how one or more of the following did this.
   a. Charles Lyell (**www.angus.gov.uk/history/features/people/lyell.htm**)
   b. Thomas Malthus (**www.bbc.co.uk/history/historic_figures/malthus_thomas.shtml**)
   c. Jean-Baptiste Lamarck (**www.bbc.co.uk/dna/h2g2/A2284210**).

3. Evolution means that humans are also evolved life forms. Find out more about one of our ancestors.

Charity

Kelly is on a huge shopping trip. She's sagging under the weight of many carrier bags full of clothes and is making her way back to the bus stop. However, she has to find her way past all the charity collectors first. One has managed to pounce on her…

Charity collector 1: Today I want to tell you all about how you can help ducks have a well-earned rest.

Kelly: Did you just say ducks?

Charity collector 1: Have you thought about how hard these ducks work all year, treading water in the pond and scooping up all our stale bread? Well, for only £1.99 a month you can help them to get away from it all…

Kelly: *[Edging away]* Sorry, I really have to catch the bus. *[Kelly moves on but after only a few steps she's stopped by another activist]*

Charity collector 2: Hi there, can I just chat to you about how you can help a child in need *[doesn't wait for Kelly to answer]* you see, some kids can't upgrade their mobile phones. It's so tragic. Some don't even have touch-screen facilities right now.

Kelly: You can't be serious – oh look, there's my bus now!

[Kelly pretends to spy her bus and breaks free. She walks a few more steps when she is intercepted by yet another collector]

Charity collector 3: It's ok, I'm not trying to get any money out of you just now. I just want you to have a think about who you'll leave your money to in your will.

Kelly: My will? I'm fourteen!

Charity collector 3: How about leaving some of your money to a new retirement home for former fashion models.

Kelly: Fashion models? You're having a laugh aren't you?

Sakter boy: No, this is serious stuff. The photoshoots, the travel, the magazines – it's a big comedown to normal life when these women hit their late twenties.

Kelly: First it's holidays for stressed out ducks, then it's upgrading kids' mobile phones and finally it's supporting those poor overpaid waifs. They don't need my money, and I'm not giving it to you!

[Kelly now does spot her bus and runs for it. She just makes it and digs into her pocket for the fare. She discovers that she is 5p short. Red-faced, she turns to the people on the bus.]

Kelly: Anyone got a spare 5p they can lend me? *[No one answers]*

Bus driver: Sorry darlin', exact fare only. Ye'll need tae get aff.

Kelly: But I've already put in all the money I have, and it's only 5p less than the fare.

Bus driver: Sorry hen, I'm no a charity and *[looks at her many shopping bags]* I dinnae think you count as one either…

Why give to charity?

There are thousands of charities, and which one you give to is really a matter of personal choice. You're likely to support one that means something to you – like a cancer charity because you know someone who has cancer, for example. People sometimes give their own money to charity and sometimes they ask other people to sponsor them to do things.

Some people give to charity because it makes them feel better about themselves. But sometimes they give because they feel guilty, or because they think it will make them look good. Maybe giving away our money helps us to become less attached to it. Perhaps people give to charity because they think that one day they might need help from that charity; or maybe they think it will make the world a safer place. But does it really matter why we give, as long as we help others?

 Active Learning

1. Find out which charities are given to by people in your class and their families. Why have they selected these charities and not others? What about your school and community – which charities does it support and why? Prepare a report of your findings.

2. How do charities spend the money they raise? Choose one charity and draw a diagram explaining what they do with every £1 they get.

3. What different ways can you give to charity? Find out what each of the following means:
   a. one-off donation
   b. charity event
   c. wills and legacies
   d. charity Christmas presents
   e. surfing the web
   f. charity credit card
   g. sponsorship
   h. vouchers
   i. charity shopping.

4. Choose one charity that your class would like to raise money for. Now organise a charity event to raise money. Perhaps you could do this across your school and introduce a bit of inter-class competition!

Talking and listening

- Would you have given Kelly the 5p?
- Was she right to refuse to help the three charities?
- What charities do people in your class give to? How much do they give? Which ones are the most popular?
- Why do people give anything to charity?

Progress Check

1. Which of the reasons for giving to charity do you think is the best one or the worst one? Why? Discuss in class. Rank them from best to worst.

2. Put these statements up in your classroom and get everyone to write whether they agree, disagree or are not sure about each one. Make sure they give a reason for their choice.
   a. 'It doesn't matter why you give to charity, as long as you do.'
   b. 'Charity begins at home.'
   c. 'People should help themselves before asking for help.'
   d. 'I wouldn't want to be given charity.'
   e. 'Charity should not be necessary – the governments should sort out the problems in the world.'

3. The National Lottery was introduced as a way to raise money for charity. Some people say that it just encourages people to gamble and that not enough of the money goes to charity. What do you think? Discuss in class.

4. Kelly was faced with some pretty strange charities. But are some charities more worthwhile than others? What do you think of the following causes?
   a. Building schools for children in Afghanistan.
   b. Raising money to support athletes going to the Olympics.
   c. Someone raising money to help them travel around the world.
   d. Providing help for people who are unemployed.
   e. Buying the *Big Issue*.
   f. Raising money to buy school equipment/books.
   g. Keeping a famous painting in a local art gallery.
   h. Supporting an animal rights organisation.
   i. Supporting a political party.

On your own

1. Lots of organisations try to make giving to charity simpler. Visit a couple of websites, such as **www.charitygiving.co.uk/donate** and **www.justgiving.com**. Find out what they do and how they do it.

2. You can now raise money for charity just by visiting certain websites. Find out about some of these websites.

3. Most of what you buy could be bought in a way that supports a charity. Almost all charities have online shops selling food, clothes and more. Choose one charity and see if it has an online shop (or an actual shop). What do you normally buy that you could buy here to help charity?

In Muslim life, it's right enough
That you should not have too much stuff
For if you do then all your wealth
Won't help you with your spiritual health
Your riches will affect your mood
If you ignore the brotherhood
For keeping wealth just isn't funny
You should be generous with your money

God is great and good to you
So you should help out others too

When someone's begging in the street
You shouldn't pass or moan or greet
Look after him, support his need
And free yourself from pride and greed
This beggar's not a pest or bother
He's your family, your spiritual brother
Give to him so he's not sad
And it will make you very glad

God is great and good to you
So you should help out others too

Think of what you spend each day
On things you need, or so you say
Like smelly things to keep you clean
Or fancy clothes in which you're seen
Then think about the bills you pay
So in your house you can still stay

For if you don't pay your gas bill
Then you'll get cold and maybe ill

God is great and good to you
So you should help out others too

Work out what you need to spend
To make sure that each end meets end
House your kids, make sure they're fed
That they have clothes and a comfy bed
Make sure their life is good and fair
Then work out how much you can share
With others who may live in a slum
Which makes their life so very glum

God is great and good to you
So you should help out others too

So when you've worked out all of that
You can give out your Zakat
All things from God above are sent
You give back 2.5 per cent
This helps out those who are in need
And you are from wealth's clutches freed
So you won't feel all posh and snooty
Cos you'll have done your holy duty

God is great and good to you
So you should help out others too

 Talking and listening

- In Islam, you should thank a street beggar for giving you the chance to help them out. What do you think of that?
- Zakat means giving 2.5 per cent of your income (after spending what you need to spend) to charity. Is this enough?
- Is it better to give a fixed amount each year or just as the need arises?
- Zakat is a duty – something you must do. Should people be 'forced' to give to charity?
- From the poem above, what might a Muslim mean by saying that Zakat is just 'giving back'?

Zakat

For a Muslim, Zakat is worked out as follows. You work out how much money you make in a year. Take away all that you have to pay in order to live without making demands on others. Then you give away 2.5 per cent of what's left. This is the absolute minimum you are expected to give, and you can give much more if you like. For a Muslim, Zakat is not an act of choice – it is a duty. Zakat is so important that it is one of the Five Pillars of Islam. Zakat is a way of giving thanks back to God for what he has given you, but it is also a way to free yourself from being too attached to money and material things. Do you think giving Zakat makes the world a better place?

Active Learning

1. Talk to your parents and work out what your Zakat would be (or is, if you're Muslim).

2. Find out about the other four Pillars of Islam – how does Zakat fit into these? Report your findings in illustrated artwork and text.

3. What should Zakat be spent on and what is it spent on? Have a look at Muslim websites such as **www.islamic-relief.org.uk/ OneStopZakatShop.aspx** and **www.muslimaid.org** for ideas. Display your findings.

4. In Islam there are special times of year (or life) when extra charity is given. These include the birth of a baby, Ramadan and Eid. Find out how much is given at these times and why, and create a short fact file.

On your own

1. Visit the website of a Muslim charity. What does it do? How does it spend its money? Where does its support come from?

2. How do Muslims in your local community give to charity other than Zakat? Are there any local projects or initiatives led by individuals?

3. Many Muslims disagree with the National Lottery as a way to raise money. Find out why and compare these reasons with your learning in the previous section. The website www.islamic-truth.co.uk/ sitefiles/short-articles/ islam-view-lottery-1.htm should help.

 **Progress Check**

1. Some Muslims say that the main aim of Zakat is to support the brotherhood (Ummah) of Islam. Others argue that Zakat should be used to help anyone, whether they are Muslim or not. What do you think? Discuss in class.

2. When something is a duty, people sometimes feel that it is a bind rather than a pleasure. If you're Muslim, what do you feel about Zakat? What different views are there in your community about it? If you're not Muslim, would you find giving Zakat a helpful thing or a nuisance?

3. In what ways do Muslims believe that 'God is good to you'? Make a list of as many things as you can.

4. Muslims believe that God judges how we spend our time and our money. How well or badly would you be judged on your use of time and money until now?

43 The Khalsa and The Salvation Army

My name is Sanjeev Singh. I am a member of the Sikh Khalsa. This means that I believe it is my duty to defend my faith and all that it stands for.

I believe that you should give a tenth of everything you have – your time, your wealth, your energy. This is called Dasvandh.

I can do this in very practical ways. It might just be sweeping someone's floor or getting something from the shops for them. It could be visiting them when they are ill, or helping them decorate their house.

Every week in our Gurdawara there is a free meal. Everyone is welcome. The food is donated, cooked and served by volunteers like me. This means that the poorest people can eat well for at least one day a week.

As a member of the Khalsa, I believe that I am a warrior. I am fighting a war against injustice, poverty and need wherever it is found. I do not do this to make me look good – or even feel good. I do it because it is right. I am making the world the way God would want it to be.

My name is Alison Stewart. I am a member of The Salvation Army. I believe that I should defend my Christian faith and all that it stands for.

I believe in giving a tenth of my income back to God. This is called tithing. I also give a lot of my time to do God's work.

Salvationism is 'Christianity with its sleeves rolled up'. We believe in showing our faith through practical works of kindness. This could be transforming a community garden or helping a homeless person find accommodation.

We have many hostels for the homeless around the world. They offer shelter, food and friendship. They also help people to deal with any problems they have and learn new skills so they can rebuild their lives and move into a home of their own.

As a Salvationist, I believe that I am fighting against poverty, suffering and injustice and bringing hope to people's lives. I do this as my way of showing love to God and thanking God for what he has given me, and also as a way of loving other people. By doing this, I believe that I can help make the world the way God would want it to be.

Talking and listening

- What things do this Sikh and this Christian have in common?
- How often do people in your class help others?
- What evidence is there in your community of people helping others?
- Is doing things for charity better than just giving money?

Fight the good fight

It might be a bit funny to think of everyday religious people engaged in battle, but members of the Khalsa and The Salvation Army think they are doing just that. Members of the Khalsa see themselves as protectors of their faith, but also of the weak, the poor and the needy. They believe that charity isn't just about giving money, it's about giving time and energy too. In the Langar kitchen, where the free meal is provided, you will find people from all walks of life standing side by side doing very ordinary tasks.

Members of The Salvation Army will also do very ordinary things for people to help them out. They reach out to the poor and those often forgotten by others by providing food, shelter and someone to talk to. The Salvation Army hostels for the homeless are well known all over the world. The Salvation Army also runs many other services, such as drug rehab centres and homes for people who have suffered abuse. Both of these groups fight for what is right. They both stress that charity is about more than just giving money. What could you do to help others?

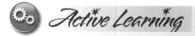

Active Learning

1. Find out how the Khalsa began. What was its original purpose? How do members of the Khalsa show that they are warriors by what they wear? Retell the story of the founding of the Khalsa as a drama or strip cartoon, or design an illustrated poster about the uniform of the Khalsa.

2. How did The Salvation Army begin with the work of William Booth in nineteenth-century London? What was its original purpose? What different uniforms do Salvationists have around the world? (And how have these changed over time?)

3. Find out what happens in the Langar kitchen and why it exists. What kind of food is served and why? Find out about the great Langar kitchen provided daily at the Golden Temple in Amritsar, the home of the Sikh faith. Perhaps with the help of your Home Economics department you could provide a Langar kitchen for a day.

→

4. Find out what work The Salvation Army does in your area, in Scotland and around the world. Have a look at **www. salvationarmy.org.uk**. Create a display board of the Salvationists' work and try to show the variety of their activities.

5. Work out how many hours a day you are awake. Now work out how much a tenth of that is. What could you do with that tenth of your time to help others? What might you be able to do in your school to help others?

Progress Check

1. Do you think that religious people should take an 'army-like' approach to their lives? Does this match up with their religious views? Do you think that the world is like a battleground between the rich and the poor? Discuss in class.

2. In the Punjab (where Sikhism began) and in Sikh communities throughout Scotland, the elderly are given special care and consideration. The Salvation Army also does a lot of work for the elderly. What are the special needs of older people? What help do they need in their lives that younger people don't? Perhaps you could interview some older people. Did you learn anything that surprised you? (If you can't interview someone, charities like Help the Aged will be able to give you some idea of the special needs of older people.)

3. Are some groups in society more deserving of help than others? Discuss your ideas and write down your views.

4. Some people say that religious people should stick to religion and not get involved in things like helping rehabilitate drug addicts or alcoholics. What do you think? Why might a religious person feel that they should be involved in anything that helps people?

On your own

1. Visit the website of Khalsa Aid (**www.khalsaaid.org**). What does this organisation do and why?

2. Visit the website of The Salvation Army (**www. salvationarmy.org.uk**). What different things does this organisation do?

3. The Khalsa provide only vegetarian food at the Langar kitchen and the Salvation Army do not allow alcohol in their hostels (or at events in their churches). Find out why.

Here are some posters from the charity Christian Aid…

Christian Aid

This organisation puts Christian beliefs into practice by helping people in the developing world to find ways out of poverty. It also responds to crisis events such as natural disasters and runs fundraising and awareness-raising events throughout the year, including a special week of fundraising called Christian Aid Week. Christian Aid believes that people should not just help the poor, but challenge those in power to do something about the causes of poverty. It was one of the organisations that campaigned to get developing world debt cancelled in the Jubilee Debt Campaign. You might have raised money for charity, but when did you last campaign on behalf of those in need?

Active Learning

1. Find out about the problem of developing world debt. What is it? How did it start in the first place? What does it mean for people in countries that have to pay this back? What part do banks and world governments play in this? What was the Jubilee 2000 campaign that tried to 'Make Poverty History'? Did it work? What more needs to be done? Prepare a report on your findings.

2. Visit the Christian Aid website (**www.christianaid.org.uk**). Find out more about what it does and why it does it. Now design a poster like the ones on page 139. Your poster should tackle one of the issues Christian Aid campaigns about in a new way.

3. Write to your MSP and find out his or her views about developing world debt. What could the Scottish and UK governments do to help? Alternatively, you could email your MSP and send some of your project work – maybe he or she will come into school and talk to you.

4. The board game Monopoly is all about trying to make as much money as you can through buying and selling property. Design a Monopoly set that is all about helping the poor. What things would change on the board? How could the game get people thinking about poverty?

5. Organise a charity event in your school. It could be to support Christian Aid or any other charity you like. It should not only raise money but also teach people about world poverty and the issues linked to it. Perhaps you could have a talent show with short video clips about world poverty between the acts? Or you could write a song to be performed in your school, like the Band Aid songs of the past.

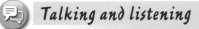

Talking and listening

- What is the message in each of the posters?
- Which poster do you think is the most effective? Why?
- Should people give to Christian Aid if they're not Christians?
- Should Christian Aid help people who are not Christians?
- Why is charity still necessary in the twenty-first century? Will it ever not be necessary?

Progress Check

1. Discuss this statement: 'Christian organisations should not be telling governments what to do.'

2. What do you think is the most effective way for organisations like Christian Aid to campaign against poverty? For each of the following ideas, write the points 'for' and 'against' this way of protesting:
   a. writing to politicians
   b. meeting with members of the government
   c. protest marches on the streets
   d. protest 'stunts'
   e. getting famous people to speak out about poverty
   f. posters and TV adverts
   g. charity concerts and big events
   h. knocking on people's doors and telling them about poverty issues
   i. boycotting products or producers
   j. selling fair-trade goods.

3. Most Christians believe that organisations like Christian Aid should help anyone, no matter what their faith is. However, some believe that Christian Aid should help Christians first. What do you think? Discuss in class.

4. A TV programme recently tried to help a charity shop improve its image. Christian Aid does not have shops, but design what your ideal Christian Aid shop (or another charity if you like) would be like.

 **On your own**

1. Design a webpage for a charity that is important to you.

2. Look back at the religions and charity organisations you have studied so far. What do they have in common? What differences do they have?

3. 'The widow's coin' is a well-known Christian story about giving. Find out about it and retell it in your own words. What is the message of this story?

45 Save the Children / Age UK

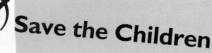

Save the Children

Consuela is nine years old. She was abandoned by her parents when she was only two. She now works on the streets of a large city in South America. She weaves in and out of busy traffic queues with a sponge in her hand to wash windscreens and hope that someone will give her a few coins for doing this. Sometimes they do, mostly they don't. It is a very dangerous job, the roads are very busy and the drivers don't always see her. Once or twice a driver has asked her to get into the car with him. She won't do this – she has heard from other girls about what can happen. Consuela has no home, unless you call an old cardboard box a home. It is sometimes cold at night and it can be very frightening too. Packs of dogs roam the streets. Consuela dreams that she lives in a big mansion, has fine clothes and a table groaning with food. She doesn't know what her future holds… or even if she has a future.

Anala is seventy-three years old. She lives in the alleyway behind a fast food restaurant in a large Asian city. Most of what she eats has been thrown out into the alleyway or raked from the dustbins.

Anala once had family, including two children, but both died in their teenage years. Her brother moved to another city, and now she does not know where he is or even if he is alive. She is completely alone in the world. Occasionally, street workers help her out for a while – but there are many people just like Anala, and there's not enough time to help everyone. Anala will not beg, but she is too frail to do any kind of work. She once made beautiful dresses, but her failing eyesight and crippled fingers mean that she can't do this any more. Sometimes Anala dreams that she is a girl again: running and laughing, playing with her friends. Anala dreams of a future where her last few years will be more comfortable, but she knows that this is unlikely…

💬 Talking and listening

■ When you are in need, does it matter what age you are?
■ In what ways is Consuela's life different from nine year olds you know?
■ In what ways is Anala's life different from any older people you know?
■ If you could help only Consuela or Anala, who would you help and why?
■ What different needs do old and young people have?

Last in Line, Last in School

How donors are failing children in conflict-affected fragile states

Save the Children Rewrite the Future

Helping people of all ages

Save the Children tries to help young people get a good start in life. Its work focuses on four areas:

1. looking after children's health – making sure that they do not die young, sometimes from illnesses that are easy to treat;

2. ensuring that they are free from hunger – many children in the world suffer from extreme forms of malnutrition that affect everything they do in life;

3. making sure they have an education – around 77 million children do not have any kind of schooling;

4. protecting children from all possible threats – being sold as slaves, or used as child soldiers. It deals with everyday problems that children face as well as special needs resulting from wars and disasters.

Age UK works on behalf of people in later life, finding out what their needs are and supporting them. The charity also campaigns to get people and governments thinking about the needs of older people, and believes that everyone should be able to live their life with dignity and have enough money to provide for their needs. People need help no matter what age they are. What could you do?

Active Learning

1. As a class, split into two groups. One group should find out about street children around the world. Why are they on the streets? What is their life like? What things can happen to them? Why are they especially vulnerable? The other group should do exactly the same in relation to homeless older people. Report and display your findings.

2. Get photos from the Internet that illustrate the problems faced by children and older people in today's world. Create an exhibition, with a caption under each photo explaining the special needs of a child or older person.

3. Design a poster for either Save the Children or Age UK.

4. Visit the websites of both organisations (**www.ageuk.org.uk** and **www.savethechildren.org.uk**). In what ways are they similar? How do they differ? How does each charity try to gain support? (You will find evidence that these organisations look after the interests of more than one age group.)

5. Organise a school event to support these charities.

1. Do you think it is more important to help those in need who are young or those who are old (or both equally?) Make a list of arguments supporting each possibility.
   a. 'I think we should help the young first because…'
   b. 'I think we should help older people first because…'
   c. 'I think we should help both equally because…'

2. What have you learned about charity that you didn't know before? Have any of your views changed? Are you more or less likely to help charities? What things do charities do well? What could they improve?

3. Go through all the religious views and other viewpoints you have explored in this unit. Get everyone in your class to write as many different endings for the following sentence as they can: 'We should help charity because…'

4. Do you think charity will ever stop being necessary? How could that wish become reality? What might stop it happening? Discuss in class and express your own views.

On your own

1. The charities you have looked at in this unit have mostly been linked to human needs. Find out about other charities that have different aims. You could look at charities that support:
   a. animal rights/issues
   b. nature/conservation issues
   c. protecting heritage.

2. In Scotland, independent (private) schools are charities. Some people argue that they should not be so. Find out about the different views held about this. What do you think?

3. In this Unit, you have looked mostly at large charities. What smaller local charities are there in your community? What could you do to help them?

Exploring ethics

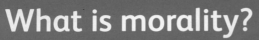

46 What is morality?

- Kyle and Ali regularly download music from the Internet and share it. One day a message flashes up on the screen warning them that they are breaking the law.

- Susan's kids like movies. One is 12 years old and the other is 11. Susan lets them watch movies that are rated at 15.

- Ian runs a shop. Young people regularly come into the shop and buy cigarettes. He doesn't ask for proof of age ID.

- Bianca finds a lottery ticket lying on the floor of a supermarket. She keeps it and finds that it is a winning ticket.

- Jane is a doctor. One night she sees two cars crash. Both drivers will die without her help, but she only has time to save one.

- You're out shopping. Your best friend takes something and hides it in her pocket.

- Owen is pretty good with computers. One day he accidentally taps into someone else's email account.

- Peter knows that one of his friends is bullying someone.

- Rachael sees someone selling drugs outside her school gates.

- Conner's standing with a group of mates. Someone has just told a joke that is in very bad taste. Everyone else laughs along.

- Kate's bank card seems to be getting money out of cash machines but it's not coming out of her account.

- Ciara is a vegetarian. She visits her auntie's house for dinner, but she doesn't know she's a veggie. Old Auntie doesn't have much money, but she has spent a lot making a lovely roast beef dinner.

- Karen's house was robbed and her student sax, which cost £200, was stolen. She's filling in the insurance claim form. Someone suggests that she claims for a much better sax than the one that was stolen.

- Tom lives in a flat and hears screaming nearby. He wonders whether or not he should phone the Police.

- A new chemical product allows you to choose the kind of child you have. Mary wants to have a baby and wonders about buying the product.

- Morgan is the leader of a country at war. His military advisers suggest that the war can be brought to a quick end with a massive bombing campaign in the enemy country. The only problem is that many civilians will die in this campaign.

- Ashley's friend has developed a problem with BO that she doesn't seem to have noticed. Ashley wonders if she should point this out to her friend.

🗨 Talking and listening

- Which of the problems above do you think are the most complicated?
- What differences of opinion are there in your class about these problems?
- Has anybody faced any of these problems in real life? What did they do?
- How do you decide what's right and what's wrong?
- Is there anything that is always right or always wrong?

What is morality?

Ethics is the study of how we make decisions about what's right and wrong. Ethical problems like these are a good way to show you what your own moral values are. From childhood, we are told stories where there are obviously 'right' decisions and 'wrong' ones. We learn what's right and wrong by following (or not) the examples that people have set us; we tend to copy behaviours that are rewarded and not ones that are punished. Sometimes we follow religious codes such as the Ten Commandments. Sometimes we just follow the laws of our country (until we think that those laws themselves might be wrong). Sometimes we do what looks like it would bring the most benefit for the greatest number of people. Sometimes we just go with our gut instinct. Deciding what's right and wrong isn't always easy – especially when those decisions might have serious effects for us and others. How do you decide what's right and wrong?

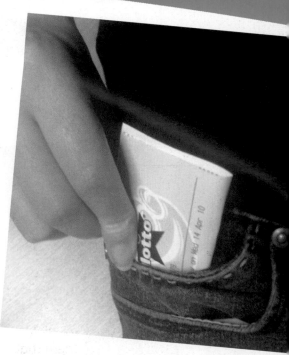

Active Learning

1. For each of the ethical problems, what would you advise the person to do? Is it the same as what you would do?

2. Working in groups, look at a selection of the ethical problems. How often do the same choices come up? How different are the choices? Why does this difference exist? Are there any that everyone agrees on? Report back as a group and say whether anyone's views were changed by the discussions.

3. People sometimes ask for more information before they make an ethical decision. Choose some of the ethical problems and explain what further information you might need before you make your decision.

4. Take one of the ethical problems and look at it in a little more detail. What would someone do if they based their moral decision-making on:
   a. self-interest
   b. the interests of others
   c. a religious view
   d. following the law
   e. what would be best for the greatest number of people
   f. the situation itself.

5. Create a class poster split into two sections. This poster should display images showing what your class thinks is 'Right' and 'Wrong'. You could use local examples, or things you have looked at in other areas of this book.

 Progress Check

1. Order the ethical problems on page 146 from 'most serious' to 'least serious'. Explain your decisions. Sit in groups and compare lists.

2. Explain how each of the following might have affected what you think is right and wrong:
   a. your parents' teaching
   b. your parents' example
   c. the example set by your peers
   d. your local community or nationality
   e. what you have learned in school
   f. your own beliefs.

3. Play a game of call my bluff. Three people in your class should explain what they would do for a number of the ethical problems. They can either tell the truth or tell lies. The class must guess whether they are telling the truth or not.

4. Design a board game based on the idea of right and wrong. For instance you could do snakes and ladders, where the snakes are wrong actions and the ladders are right actions.

🗨️ *On your own*

1. Look through some magazines aimed at people of your age. Cut out and display items that describe or suggest things you think are wrong. Explain your choice.

2. Ask your parents and older relatives what they think about right and wrong these days. How do the values that people have in the twenty-first century compare with those of older generations? Report your findings to the class.

3. Many of the moral problems you have looked at in this section have rather fancy names and a long history. Look up one or more of the following on the Internet and see what you find:
   a. utilitarianism
   b. legalism
   c. situation ethics
   d. Kantian ethics
   e. moral relativism / absolutism.

Bahá'í Faith

Lay not on any soul a load that you would not wish to be laid upon you, and desire not for anyone the things you would not desire for yourself.

Bahá'u'lláh, **Gleanings**

Buddhism

Treat not others in ways that you yourself would find hurtful.

The Buddha, **Udana-Varga 5.18**

Christianity

In everything, do to others as you would have them do to you; for this is the law and the prophets.

Jesus, **Matthew 7:12**

Confucianism

One word which sums up the basis of all good conduct… loving-kindness. Do not do to others what you do not want done to yourself.

Confucius, **Analects 15.23**

Hinduism

This is the sum of duty: do not do to others what would cause pain if done to you.

Mahabharata 5:1517

Islam

Not one of you truly believes until you wish for others what you wish for yourself.

The Prophet Muhammad, **Hadith**

Jainism

One should treat all creatures in the world as one would like to be treated.

Mahavira, **Sutrakritanga 1.11.33**

Judaism

What is hateful to you, do not do to your neighbour. This is the whole Torah; all the rest is commentary. Go and learn it.

Hillel, **Talmud, Shabbath 31a**

Native Spirituality

We are as much alive as we keep the earth alive.

Chief Dan George

Sikhism

I am a stranger to no one; and no one is a stranger to me. Indeed, I am a friend to all.

Guru Granth Sahib, p.1299

Taoism

Regard your neighbour's gain as your own gain and your neighbour's loss as your own loss.

Lao Tzu, **T'ai Shang Kan Ying P'ien, 213-218**

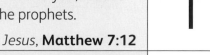

Unitarianism

We affirm and promote respect for the interdependent web of all existence of which we are a part.

Unitarian principle

Source: **www.scarboromissions.ca/Golden_rule/sacred_texts.php**.

- What do all of the quotations on page 149 have in common?
- Which one do you think is the best? Why?
- Do you agree or disagree with any of the quotations?
- Why do you think these are called the golden rule?
- Do you follow the golden rule?

The golden rule

Don't like someone sticking a pencil up your nose? Then don't do it to anyone else. Like people sharing their chocolate with you? Then share yours. This is the golden rule. It's a simple enough rule really, and a version of it appears in pretty much every culture, religion and belief system in the world. So, before you make any decision about right and wrong, you have to ask yourself how it would affect you if someone else made the decision you're about to make.

Of course, it's not that simple. A famous atheist philosopher called Bertrand Russell once said 'Do not do to others what you would have them do to you: their tastes may not be the same.' And there's the problem. What you absolutely love, someone else might absolutely hate and vice versa. However, maybe even thinking about how our actions might affect others would make the world a better place. What do you think?

![active learning icon] *Active Learning*

1. Take three or four of the quotations and illustrate them in your own way, according to the faith or viewpoint they are linked to.

2. Following a discussion in class, draw up a golden rule charter that would reflect what people in your class would not like done to them. Try to structure your list so that the most serious ones are at the top and the least serious ones at the bottom. How right was Bertrand Russell? Are people's tastes very different? Display your charter.

3. List four or five things that you would like people to do for you. Now ask the rest of your class which of your things they would also like. Again, display your findings – how much do people have in common in terms of their likes and dislikes?

4. Plan, organise and run a golden rule day in your school. On this day, people should try to do things for others that they would like done to them and avoid doing things they wouldn't like. Design posters, or maybe hold an assembly, to explain the idea behind the day. How difficult or easy would this be?

5. Look through a couple of newspapers (tabloids might be quite good for this). Choose one story and rewrite it as if the people involved had decided to follow the golden rule.

1. Discuss these statements and note the different viewpoints raised:
   a. 'A world where everyone followed the golden rule would be perfect.'
   b. 'Even if you tried to follow the golden rule, what you meant to happen might not be what actually happens.'
   c. 'If everybody followed the golden rule then you would have to make up right and wrong as you go along according to different people's likes and dislikes. That's impossible.'

2. Imagine you decided to follow the golden rule (or your government did), and you discovered a small group of people who like to be killed and eaten when they reach the age of twenty-five. If you followed the golden rule, would you have to agree to do this for them? Is it right? Discuss in class.

3. Write your own poem explaining what the golden rule is and how difficult it is to put into practice.

4. Unless the person or thing you are acting towards can express their preferences, it is very difficult to apply the golden rule. For each of the following, explain why the golden rule might be difficult to apply:
   a. in relation to animal rights
   b. in relation to people with severe learning difficulties
   c. in relation to how we treat the environment
   d. in relation to the enemy in a war situation
   e. in relation to very young babies.

On your own

1. The golden rule is expressed on page 149 according to major religions / belief systems and moral viewpoints. See if you can find more examples of how the golden rule is expressed. (See www. religioustolerance.org/reciproc.htm for some further ideas.)

2. The psychological theory of 'reciprocal altruism' supports the idea of the golden rule as a behaviour that humans have evolved to help them survive. Find out about this theory and the evidence surrounding it.

3. Look back at your work on animal rights. If we followed the golden rule, would everyone have to become a vegan?

How do you know what's right and wrong?

I am a Christian person and I know what's wrong and right
For everything I do each day, is done within God's sight
So when I make decisions, about what's right or true
I just ask myself the question, 'Now what would Jesus do?'

And me, I am a Muslim and a very holy man
I learn what's right and what is wrong by reading the Koran
So from the words of God himself, my moral teachings draw
Themselves into a code of life in the Shariah Law

Jewish scholars have for long discussed and said 'blah bah'
It might mean this, it might mean that, but if it's in Torah
Then it supports us in our lives, and is our guiding light
It covers everything there is, and shows us what is right

We Buddhists have a simple way to work out what is good
Like how to treat the world around, and how not to be rude
We have our books like others too, all laid upon the shelf
But Buddha said 'Don't stick to a book – work it out for yourself'

In Hinduism too we have our books, which tell us what is good
Though we also learn the stories of our faith that show what should
Be done so that we're doing good, and avoiding all that's bad
So that our world is a good place, not mad or sad, but glad

We Sikhs avoid wrongdoing and no kindnesses we lack
Through following the teachings of our Gurus like Nanak
Our holy book has guidance, as long as it is read
Though every night we tuck it up and send it off to bed

In Humanism we don't have scriptures, prayers or God
But we live just as morally, and you shouldn't think that's odd
We get no guidance from on high – of this we have no need
We make up our own minds what's right – that's our only creed

But on one thing we're all agreed, to save our world from blight
We must avoid wrongdoing and aim to do what's right
For though we have our different ways of finding out what's true
We try to live as best we can, while helping others too

Talking and listening

- How do you work out what is right and wrong?
- What things do these faiths/viewpoints have in common when deciding what's right and wrong?
- Is there such a thing as 'the truth'?
- Should people follow the teachings of others in deciding what's right?
- Should people turn to books and stories to help them decide what's right?

How your beliefs affect your values

Your values are the ways that you approach decisions about right and wrong. They're not just affected by where you live and who your parents are – they can also be affected by your beliefs. Most countries have laws and ways of doing things that are linked to the major beliefs present in that country. But what exactly do we mean by beliefs affecting our values?

Many religions have holy books that show their followers what's right and wrong. Many religious people follow the traditions of their faith – values passed down through the ages – and some follow the example of key figures in their faith. Non-religious people work out their values using their own reasoning. Whatever you believe or don't believe, it will affect how you live your life. How do your beliefs affect your values?

 Active Learning

1. Find out what the Ten Commandments are. Which ones do you think apply in today's world? You could create a display about the Ten Commandments and use examples from the news of where they are still kept or ignored.

2. Choose one of the holy books below and find examples of their teaching about right and wrong. Using words from the holy books, create an exhibition about values. Choose from:
   a. the Koran
   b. the Torah
   c. the Talmud
   d. the Bhagavad Gita
   e. the Upanishads
   f. the Christian New Testament
   g. the Guru Granth Sahib
   h. the Tao te ching.

3. Choose one or more of the following religious figures and create a fact file explaining how their life and teachings set an example about living a good life:
   a. Muhammad
   b. Jesus
   c. the Gurus of Sikhism
   d. Moses
   e. Abraham
   f. Buddha shakyamuni
   g. Krishna
   h. Rama.

→

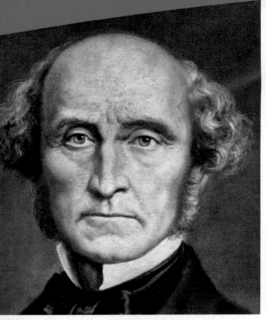

John Stuart Mill

4. Many non-religious people try to live their life in a moral way, but of course they don't use the teachings of a faith to help them. Choose one or more of the following and find out what their views are about morality.
   a. the Humanist Society of Scotland (**www.humanism-scotland. org.uk**)
   b. the British Humanist Association (**www.humanism.org.uk/ home**)
   c. the utilitarian John Stuart Mill (**www.utilitarianism.com/jsmill. htm**)
   d. the modern utilitarian Peter Singer (**www.princeton. edu/~psinger**).

 On your own

1. Design a quiz that aims to find out how moral a person is and where they get their morality from. You could make up some scenarios and ask people what they would do. Their answers should be confidential. Do religious people seem to be more moral than non-religious people, or is it the other way round?

2. What is right and wrong sometimes changes over time. Talk to a History teacher and come up with one value or attitude that has changed over the years. What is acceptable today that might not have been acceptable fifty, 100 or 200 years ago?

3. How do you think morality might change in the future? Will people become less or more moral? What things might become 'stricter' or 'less strict'?

Progress Check

1. Religious people generally obey the laws of the country they live in. What should a religious person do if the laws of their country contradict their religious values? Discuss in class.

2. Religious people follow the teachings of their faith, but sometimes this isn't easy. What should a religious person do in the following situations?
   a. Their holy book says nothing about a particular moral problem (like a scientific ethical issue).
   b. Their holy book seems to say contradictory things about a moral issue.
   c. It is not clear what one of their key religious figures would have done.
   d. They pray and their God seems to be telling them to do something that they think is very wrong.
   e. Their religious leaders advise them to break the law or do things that are wrong.

3. What are the top three moral rules that all religions would agree on?

4. Look at the ethical issues at the start of the previous section. Answer each one according to one or more of the religions / non-religious views you have explored in this section.

My name is John. I fought in the Second World War. I saw active service, and yes, I killed people. I don't think I ever understood about the politics of it all, I just knew that we had to stop Hitler. They were the enemy and that's just the way things were. Do I lose any sleep over it? No. War isn't pretty, but you've got to do what's needed.

My name is Terry. I did not fight in the Second World War and they put me in prison for it. I was not prepared to help the military activities in any way – even as a non-combatant. In prison, they thought I was just a coward and they treated me like dirt. It wasn't much better when I got out: people would spit on me in the street. Would I do it again? Certainly – I will never take the life of another human being.

My name is Stuart. I fought in the Second World War. I saw active service and yes, I killed people. I still wake some nights and see their faces. No, I didn't really understand what I was fighting for, and yes, I now wish I had never signed up. Bullets flew all around me and my mates fell and died by my side. I just wish the leaders had done more to prevent the war.

My name is George. I was a conscientious objector during the Second World War, but I went into battle unarmed as a medic. I pulled men away from the battlefield, and I would have saved one of the enemy if I had been able to. I was not going to kill someone just because my government told me to. Some of the other soldiers thought I was a coward, but others respected the fact that I stood up for what I believed in.

THEIR NAME LIVETH FOR EVERMORE

The taking of human life

Most people agree that it is wrong to take human life without good reason, but some think that war is a good enough reason. Even religious people seem to accept the taking of life during wars as something that just has to be done. Humans have a long history of warring with each other, and right now there are likely to be wars or conflicts going on somewhere around the world. Ordinary people can find themselves given the right to kill other ordinary people. But there are some who believe that no human should ever take another human's life. Would you kill others in a war if you had to?

Talking and listening

- Is it ever right to kill a human being?
- Why do we seem to accept the idea of killing during wars?
- Should there be rules in wars?
- What do you think of people who refuse to fight in wars?
- What wars and conflicts are going on in the world today?

Active Learning

1. The philosopher Erasmus said that war is terrible because all our normal behaviours get turned on their head. Carry out the following survey in your class and report your findings.

	Yes	No	Not sure
Is it right to kill people?			
Is it right to kill people in war?			
Is it right to destroy property?			
Is it right to destroy property during war?			
Is it right to lie?			
Is it right to lie during war?			
Is it right to kill yourself in order to kill others?			
Is it right to kill yourself in a war in order to kill others?			

Erasmus said that all the non-war questions would get a No and all the war questions would get a Yes – does your class agree?

2. Find out about one war from the past and one conflict that is going on right now. Answer the following questions about each one:
   a. What was the reason for it and who was involved?
   b. What kind of fighting took place?
   c. How many died? How many soldiers / civilians?
   d. Who objected to the war and why?
   e. Do you think it was right to go to war in this situation?

3. Here are some of the rules of war. Discuss each one in relation to one of the wars in the last task. How many were broken?
   a. You should only use as much force as is necessary.
   b. You should try to avoid killing civilians.
   c. Prisoners of war should be treated well.
   d. Attacks should have a specific target.

4. Conscientious objectors refuse to fight in wars. Some, like George, do not fight but help out in other ways; others, like Terry, refuse to have anything to do with war and are sometimes sent to prison. Find out about conscientious objectors. Why did they refuse to fight? How did people treat them? What happened to them? What do you think about their actions? Design an illustrated information sheet showing your findings.

5. Imagine a war broke out tomorrow that Scotland entered. Now imagine that you are an age where you could be called up to fight. What would you do? Would any of the following things make a difference to your decision?
   a. who the war was against
   b. whether Scotland was fighting back, supporting another country or starting the war
   c. what job you were asked to do in the war
   d. what the chances of you being in actual combat were.
   Discuss these in class and see what range of viewpoints and beliefs there are.

Progress Check

1. Discuss the following statements:
   a. 'War is always wrong.'
   b. 'There can be good reasons for going to war.'
   c. 'In war, anything goes.'
   d. 'There will always be wars – it's human nature.'
   e. 'People should refuse to fight in wars – then they wouldn't happen.'

2. Here are some reasons why countries go to war. Put them into order, with the one you think is the 'best' at the top. Why have you ordered them like this? What differences are there in your class?
   a. defending your country from attack by another country
   b. defending your way of life
   c. helping out another country
   d. getting more land or resources for your country
   e. getting land back that your government says is rightfully yours.

3. Some people say that modern war is much worse than war in the past because we now have weapons of mass destruction (WMDs), like biological or nuclear weapons. Look back at the rules of war. Do WMDs break any of these rules? Should we have them? Have a class debate.

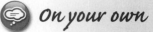 On your own

1. Choose one religion you have studied this year and find out about its views on war. See www.ppu.org.uk/learn/infodocs/st_religions.html for ideas.

2. Find out about some films about war. Did they present war as glorious or terrible? How 'realistic' were they? See the list of top 50 war movies at www.imdb.com/chart/war.

3. Pro- and anti-war propaganda have been a feature of wars for some time now. Have a look at some propaganda. What messages do they express about war? Simply type in 'pro war posters' or 'anti war posters' into Google Images.

On a sphere of matter there is a thin skin. Above this skin there is an equally thin layer of atmosphere. Just below this thinnest of skins, life cannot exist. Above and beyond this atmosphere, life cannot exist – at least as we know it. Should the temperature of this finely balanced thing increase or decrease by just a small amount, then life as we know it might come to an end. Should a stray piece of space rock come into contact with this sphere, then life as we know it would come to an end. Should the gases in this atmosphere change in only small ways, or the land and the oceans become poisoned, then life as we understand it might come to an end. This sphere has energy and resources that cannot last forever. Even the Sun, upon which this sphere depends for its existence, cannot live forever.

Tip the scales slightly one way or another and the whole thing falls apart. The trees that balance out the oxygen in the atmosphere are disappearing fast. The water they held in the soil washes away, leaving only deserts. The ice-capped frozen lands of the north and south reflect back the sunlight, keeping the temperature just right. As they melt, the sunlight warms us up yet more. The land is farmed to exhaustion and cannot recover, becoming wasted and useless. The seas become choked with what we leave behind and life within it dies. We remove its life forms for our own use and they cannot recover.

Yet on this sphere, life tries to cling on to every possible foothold. Wherever you go, living things can be found. In the deepest oceans, in the cauldrons of volcanoes, in the coldest places imaginable, things survive. But for how long?

Seen from space, the Earth is but a tiny blue dot in a vast universe whose size we can't even begin to imagine. And yet there is life here – dazzling in its variety, amazing in its adaptability, astounding in its beauty. We have one planet that we call home. You would think we would want to look after it.

The rights of nature

You probably recycle your bottles and don't use plastic carrier bags. You maybe cycle to school instead of getting a lift in a car. Perhaps you buy only environmentally friendly products. Perhaps you don't. Humans are changing the environment by their lives and actions – and not always in a good way. Nature is a finely balanced system where everything depends on everything else.

Talking and listening

- What do you do to look after nature?
- Is it important to care for nature?
- What evidence is there of humans causing changes in nature?
- How important are environmental issues to people in your class?
- Whose responsibility is it to look after the environment?

We're starting to realise that humans have a very big impact on the natural world. Pretty much everybody now knows about the most common environmental issues, and most people try to live a life that is helpful to the environment. But are we just mucking about with the superficial things? Are we really living environmentally friendly lives? Governments can make laws and agree programmes to help nature, but if people don't change their individual lifestyles, then what's the use?

Do you value nature? How do you show it? What will happen if you don't?

Active Learning

1. Create a project on one of the following environmental issues. Make sure that you include: what the main issue is; facts and opinions about the issue; how it has come about; what we can do to put it right. You might want to work with your Geography and Science departments on this:
   a. global climate change
   b. destruction of the rainforests (or other natural habitats)
   c. pollution of oceans / land / air
   d. over-use of natural resources (for example over-fishing, ore extraction etc)
   e. energy creation.
   In this task you could use some movies about environmental disasters, such as *The Day After Tomorrow*.

2. Carry out a survey of how environmentally friendly your school is. You could look at the following issues:
   a. energy use
   b. use of other resources, such as paper etc
   c. use of cleaning materials and other chemicals
   d. how people get to school
   e. the food that is served.
   Create a report of your findings and explore how your school could become more environmentally friendly. At the end of your project, meet with your Head Teacher and agree on some things that your school could do to become more environmentally friendly.

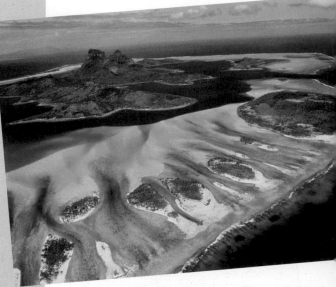

3. Design either a poster or a short TV commercial that encourages people to live in a more environmentally friendly way.

→

1. Find out about the work of one organisation that tries to protect the environment. What does it do and why? For example, see www.foe.co.uk and www.greenpeace.org.uk.

2. Find out about one religious and non-religious viewpoint about protecting nature. How similar or different are they? For example, see www.christian-ecology.org.uk, www.religionandecology.org and www.greenparty.org.uk.

3. Look through one newspaper. How many articles are there about protecting the environment? You could do this over the course of a week. Does what you find suggest that people care enough about nature?

4. On a world map, mark out areas and places where the environment is under threat. For each one, explain what the problem is and how it is linked to human activity. Try to make this as locally relevant as possible – for example, if you live in a fishing community you could look at environmental issues linked to the fishing industry.

5. Imagine Ingledoink the alien (from chapters 21, 24 and 27) arrived for another of his visits to find out what we humans get up to. What report might he bring back to his home planet about how we treat nature?

Progress Check

1. One of the problems with the rights of nature is that they sometimes come into conflict with the rights of people. For example, the problem of over-fishing might have to be balanced against the needs of fishing communities to work and survive. Choose one of the issues you have looked at and explain how people might be / are affected by this. Draw up a list of arguments for and against the changes that would be necessary to protect nature.

2. Do you think there is one environmental issue that is more important than another? Look at the environmental issues you have explored during this section and discuss as a class – try to come to some agreement about which one(s) should be tackled first.

3. Think about your own actions. What changes could you make in your life to help sort out one or more environmental issue?

4. Have a debate in class based on the following statement: 'Humans come first; nature can sort itself out as it always has.'